SEVEN FIGURE DECISIONS

SEVEN FIGURE DECISIONS

HAVING THE BALLS TO SUCCEED

NICK VERTUCCI

LIONCREST
PUBLISHING

SEVEN FIGURE DECISIONS
Having the Balls to Succeed

ISBN   978-1-61961-834-3 *Hardcover*
       978-1-61961-833-6 *Paperback*
       978-1-61961-832-9 *Ebook*

CONTENTS

FOREWORD

BY KEVIN HARRINGTON

I could hear the crowd in the hotel banquet room cheering from halfway down the hall. Their applause was thunderous. Their enthusiasm contagious. They were eager to learn. They wanted to make money. They were fired up. Something or someone was inspiring that audience in a visceral, uplifting way.

I knew I wanted to be a part of it.

Upon entering the room, I could see Nick Vertucci up on stage, sharing his wealth of knowledge about real estate investing, business, and life. I first met Nick in 2013 through a friend. I had heard about him and about what he was doing, and I wanted to know more. Now, years later, Nick is my go-to guy for real estate investing and advice. We also share a love of fine cigars, and Nick has even invited me up on stage several times to speak to his students.

Nick has a gift for teaching, inspiring, and motivating thousands of students in his Nick Vertucci Real Estate Academy. The people who attend his events come from all over the country. They're business executives, salespeople, doctors and nurses, factory workers, Realtors, bankers, homemakers, hospitality workers, and everything in between. But they all have two things in common: an entrepreneurial spirit and a desire to make money and secure their financial future by investing in real estate.

These students could not have chosen a more qualified teacher. Nick has personally done hundreds of millions of dollars in real estate deals, and his students have collectively invested in thousands of properties. No one in America knows more about residential real estate investment strategies and instruction than Nick. Some say he redefined the real estate training industry. Others call him a pioneer and a trailblazer. But he is much more than just a real estate guru.

Nick exemplifies the essence of the entrepreneurial spirit. He doesn't take no for an answer. He persists, sometimes to the point of being borderline obnoxious. But that's what it takes to build a multimillion-dollar business from nothing, especially in the crowded real estate space.

He hasn't built just one multimillion-dollar business. He didn't succeed only in the field of real estate. Like me, Nick has founded and grown multiple companies in different industries. That's not easy. It takes a set of core values, principles, and processes that can be replicated to achieve success again and again in totally different businesses. Anybody can be lucky once, but it's the serial entrepreneurs who do it over and over whom you should listen to.

That's not even what I admire most about Nick. What is most impressive is how he overcame massive setbacks and obstacles throughout his life and career and ended up back on top. He's done this not just once but many times. Each time he faced a brick wall, he either climbed over it or smashed his way through it.

The setbacks and obstacles for Nick were numerous. His father died when he was a boy. Nick struggled academically. His education didn't go past high school. And he had no technical or business training. But by sheer will and work ethic, he built a technology company from nothing into a major player in the computer industry. At one point, he had a 25,000-square-foot facility, 100 employees, and almost $40 million in revenue.

But then the tech crash of 2000 hit his interests hard.

Nick literally lost everything. He went from rolling in money and buying expensive sports cars and expensive cigars to being broke, unemployed, and millions of dollars in debt. He had a family, but he nearly lost the family home to foreclosure.

Nick suffered through some really tough and bitter years after that. Most people would have given up, but not Nick. He was determined to make a comeback. But how?

Through the lean years after his business failed, Nick noticed that one part of his personal balance sheet was still doing well. Of all of his assets, his house was the only one to increase in value even though the tech industry was burning down, the bank was calling in his loans, and his company was pretty much taken away from him. The value of his house kept going up, up, up.

A few years before the crash, Nick's wife had convinced him to upgrade their family home to a much larger house in a better neighborhood. He paid about $500,000 for it. Today, it's worth close to $1.8 million.

That lesson was not lost on Nick. He witnessed real estate's potential for appreciation in a dramatic way. That's when Nick decided to pursue a career in real estate. At first, it was a bumpy ride filled with obstacles, bitter betrayal, and heartbreak.

But I'll let Nick tell you that story—it's a good one. You'll read it later in this book. I also think you'll enjoy reading about the many setbacks and how Nick persevered, overcame, and built another incredible business.

If you're an aspiring entrepreneur, if you've suffered setbacks or betrayals, if you've ever dreamed of working for yourself, if you want to buy and sell real estate, if you want to build a solid financial future, if you need to be inspired, or if you just like great comeback stories, then you've picked up the right book.

I can vouch for my friend Nick Vertucci, and I can vouch for this book. You're going to enjoy it.

KEVIN HARRINGTON
ORIGINAL SHARK ON ABC'S *SHARK TANK*

INTRODUCTION

Self-help programs and books are popular because they inspire readers to achieve more. That's great. I'm all for that, but most self-help books fail in two critical areas when it comes to making money and business. Both of those areas I have addressed in this book.

First, most self-help books focus entirely on mindset, but they don't provide a realistic vehicle that readers can utilize to achieve financial success. As a result, the reader gets all pumped up and inspired to take action, but then they don't know what to do next. They don't know what action to take. Maybe they want to start a business or make more money while keeping their day job, but the path forward is a mystery.

You can have the most positive outlook in the world, a great attitude, a prosperity mindset, incredible willpower, and powerful success habits, but if you don't have a financial engine to put those things together, you won't achieve anything. You need something to get you there.

In this book, I recommend a money-making vehicle that has created more wealth than perhaps anything in the world. What's even better is that practically anyone can utilize this vehicle to supplement their income and build wealth. You don't need a background in business; you don't even need a college degree. I didn't graduate from college; I barely made it out of high school. But I've made a fortune nonetheless. You can too.

Second, most self-help books are based on theory rather than on the author's actual experience. The reader is expected to accept as gospel what the author is promoting in his book without any proof that it works or that the author actually used those principles in his own life and came out successful on the other side.

When I read self-help books, I'm a skeptic. I find myself questioning the author's credibility by asking, "How do you know this works? Did you use these principles in your own life? Tell me exactly what you went through and how the principles in your book helped you." Few authors connect the theory in their self-help books to their own experience. Instead, they base their advice on "research," which could mean just about anything, including secondhand stories or news articles they read somewhere.

This book destroys that model.

Everything you are about to read—from the incredible story of rags to riches to rags to riches again, to betrayal, lawsuits, and even death threats—is 100 percent my story. It happened to me. I lived through it. I didn't read about this story in a library or some business school case study; it's the story of my life, a story of a real-life grind to financial success!

As a result, the strong mind principles I write about in this book are the same ones that helped me through some of the toughest times you can imagine. I didn't conduct an academic survey to ask millionaires how they became wealthy. Instead, I overcame incredible obstacles and used the principles in this book to become wealthy myself.

I did not know the success principles in this book when I began my career. I never went to business school, and I don't read *Forbes* or *Fortune*. My father wasn't a business tycoon. In fact, he died when I was ten years old. The lessons I write about in this book I learned the hard way, by walking through fire, getting severely burned, getting back up, and walking through fire again. When you do that enough times in business, you learn some powerful lessons. Those are the lessons in this book, and every one of them comes directly from my own experience.

Most of the stories in this book are deeply personal and under normal circumstances would be kept private. You'll see what I mean starting in the first chapter and especially in chapter 6. The reason I'm giving you these personal details isn't because I want to tell you stories. I'm giving you these details because I want you to understand the truth behind the lessons. I want you to know why I'm on stage in front of hundreds of students every month training them to change their most powerful asset—their mind—and giving them a vehicle to achieve success by investing in real estate. I show them how to do both and how I personally got there myself.

I want you to understand how it happened, because then you can take that information and use it as motivation and a guide in your own life. You can say to yourself, "This guy didn't make any excuses, and look what he went through, so maybe I shouldn't make excuses either. Maybe things aren't as bad as I'm making them in my head. I'm finally going to live my life and not live somebody else's life."

I'M FINALLY GOING TO LIVE MY LIFE AND NOT LIVE SOMEBODY ELSE'S LIFE.

Many successful people plowed their way to success, tearing and clawing a path for themselves through the rocks and debris of disappointment and disaster. That's what I did too, and that's what I want you to understand. That is the reason for this book.

I don't want you to feel sorry for me because of what I went through to get here. I don't even want you to think it's just a cool story about overcoming adversity. Instead, I want to show you how I achieved success so you understand what it's going to take for you to achieve it. You'll know that no matter what life throws at you, you can overcome it and achieve success if you want it bad enough.

Before you begin reading chapter 1, let me be really clear: this book reflects what I went through and who I am as a person and a businessman. When picking the subtitle for this book, *Having the Balls to Succeed*, I was advised that I may isolate some readers with that title and that it could hurt the sales of the book. I want to be clear: I am not writing this book for sales or revenue because I am already set financially. My goal isn't to please every reader. I am writing this book from my heart and my gut and to help people succeed in business and in life like I did. I always go with my gut, and I am always real as to who I am and how I do business and live life. In chapter 6, this book gets really real, and I expose a deeply personal situation relevant to my success. At times, it is raw, and some language may get dicey. If you can handle that, read on. You won't regret it.

CHAPTER ONE

MENTORSHIP

I have always admired NBA basketball legend Michael Jordan, not just for his aggressive style of play on the court or for all his accomplishments in professional sports, including six NBA championships. I have a great affinity for Michael because he had a wonderful mentor relationship with his father and then tragically lost that mentor in the prime of both of their lives.

I know what that's like.

Michael's father, James R. Jordan, was known for mentoring and guiding his son throughout his incredible sports career, both as a child and in the early days and during his pro career with the Chicago Bulls.

James was the driving force behind Michael's success. Among other things, he instilled in his son a strong work ethic, a desire to achieve big things, and the belief that anything is possible if you set a goal, create a plan, believe in yourself, and then work toward your goal every day. Simply put, Michael Jordan was a player of pure grit and determination.

But the loving mentorship between one of the greatest athletes of all time and his father was tragically cut short. On a hot July day in 1993, James Jordan was driving home from a funeral. He had pulled over on Route 74 south of Lumberton, North Carolina, to take a rest. While he was asleep in the driver's seat, two violent criminals noticed the Lexus that Michael had purchased for his dad. The criminals shot James Jordan to death while he slept and stole the car. This happened eight days before James's fifty-seventh birthday.

THE IMPORTANCE OF MENTORSHIP

My father had me late in life. He was fifty years old when I was born, and he was the most important force in my life. He was the best father and mentor a boy could have, and I would rather spend time with him than any of my friends. I couldn't wait for him to pick me up from school every day. My father was my role model and my best friend.

The benefit of my father's age was that he had already retired from full-time work by the time I was growing up, and that paid big dividends for me. We spent almost all our time together. I was really into baseball as a kid, and he was my coach. He was not just at every game but also every practice. He coached me in much more than batting, throwing, and catching. He taught me how to succeed by working hard and thinking big. He gave me the "never give up or give in" attitude I have today.

He coached my physical and mental game. He taught me how to set my mind on something and then go after it with hard work and focus—not just stealing bases and winning games but also in other areas of life, such as my schoolwork, family, and friends.

One of his favorite sayings was, "When you do something, you do it right." He also taught me mental toughness, persistence, self-confidence, optimism, self-discipline, courage, and integrity. Those were the values he built into me from a young age, and I followed them.

"WHEN YOU DO SOMETHING, YOU DO IT RIGHT."

I applied the lessons and work ethic he taught me to sports. We spent weekends at the batting cages, working on my swing. After every practice, I remember fielding ground balls with my father until after dark, long after the other kids on the team had gone home. When I complained and asked him if we could stop, he'd say, "That's up to you.

Do you want to be the best? If so, let's keep practicing. If you want to be the best, then you have to put in more work than everyone else." It was a lesson well taught.

With my father's coaching and guidance, I became the best player on the teams I played on. I excelled on the field and off; I was often the MVP. The other players looked up to me. They asked me for advice and tried to emulate me. I had developed supreme confidence in my own abilities, and it showed—and it was all due to my father's advice and instruction.

I didn't know it then, but my father was providing me with the priceless gift of mentorship. He was the first and best mentor I ever had. We were inseparable; we were a team. He wasn't just my father; he was also my light, and I loved him dearly.

Then suddenly, when I was ten years old, my father passed away from a heart attack. I was devastated.

LACK OF MENTORSHIP

After my father passed, everything changed. After the initial shock of his death, as I slowly climbed out of a dark hole of sadness, depression, and loss, I slipped into something almost as awful: a cloud of mediocrity and self-doubt. I missed my dad more than any words could express. We had spent almost every day together for my whole life, but he was gone now, and so was his daily influence on my behavior.

Without my mentor coaching me, rooting for me, teaching me, having my back, and standing behind me, my athletic ability began to slip. My confidence slowly eroded, and I stopped putting in the work and effort it takes to stay on top. The mental toughness my father taught me began to soften. I lost my edge. After a couple of years, his absence became obvious, not just to me but also to my teammates.

Even though I was the same physically, my success on the field suffered. The other players began to catch up and overtake me, and I was no longer the MVP. I began to taste failure, and I hated it. The more I failed, the more confidence I lost. My mentor was not there to catch me or help me. But back then, I had no idea why all this was happening.

This downward spiral continued from age ten into my teens. I kept playing sports, but I did it half-assed.

I started hanging around with the wrong crowd. I grew my hair long, and I began screwing off in school. I completely lost my ability to focus, set goals, persist through setbacks, and take risks. The lessons my father taught me faded.

I started not caring about anything, or at least acting like

I didn't care. Looking back now, as an adult, I realize that not caring is actually a defense mechanism. It's a form of self-protection that prevents us from feeling the awful emotions of failure. If you don't care, you don't try, so you never fail. Right? So wrong! You may be masking the pain, but you're still feeling it and building negative internal patterns.

The pain I felt from losing my father was multiplied by losing my mentor as well. All the positive, success-enabling characteristics I had developed fell away. I became like every other rudderless kid: insecure with no goals, no drive, no lust for success, and no work ethic. I developed a bad attitude and a negative mental outlook.

THE RISE OF VICTIMHOOD

It was a difficult time, and it's painful to look back on. But today, I refuse to be a victim or act like one. I reject the victimhood mentality that is so prevalent in our society today. It seems like too many people blame their past or their parents or their lack of money or the government or any number of other excuses for not going after their dreams and succeeding in life. I reject that concept outright. The thing about the past is that you cannot change it. All you can do is learn from it and look toward the future.

Everyone eventually loses their parents and suffers heartbreak, pain, and loss. I mourned my father, I cried over him a thousand times, and I missed him so bad that it physically hurt. But that was my journey. Those were the cards I was dealt. I sit back and listen to grown men make excuses for their lack of success these days. I often hear statements such as, "I lost my father, and I haven't been the same since." Or, "My father wasn't there for me, so I have had no role model." OK, yes, I understand that it's painful, but give me a break! Quit making excuses and man up.

QUIT MAKING EXCUSES AND MAN UP.

As an adult, I know that life must go on. But as a young boy, I didn't understand that. I didn't know how to go on or what direction to go in. I paid the price for that.

RUDDERLESS YOUTH

I began to get into trouble at school. I spent a lot of time in detention, I started using drugs, and I acted out and rebelled against authority. In sports, I was just going through the motions. I was not really committed like I would be today if given that chance again. To this day, it's one of my biggest regrets because I had so much potential.

When you don't have a good mentor, it's much, much harder to persevere, to push through fear, to stay on track, to believe in yourself, and to set and achieve goals. Isolation tends to reinforce feelings of self-doubt. Without a mentor, those negative thoughts can be like a runaway freight train, almost unstoppable. When you're going at it alone, there's no one there to pick you up when you fall down—and everyone falls down. There's no one to guide you in the right direction.

But with a mentor, fears and negative thoughts can be turned around, especially when your mentor is someone who has accomplished what you are trying to accomplish. Positive role models can inspire and embolden us to make our own big moves.

When you have a mentor, you have someone to lean on when times are tough. The best mentors are people who have already achieved whatever it is that you are trying to achieve. For example, I'm extremely successful in business and in real estate investing. I've done millions of dollars in deals, and I've successfully run multiple different businesses. So I'm a great mentor and coach in both areas—owning and running a business and real estate investing. If you want to be a football quarterback, then your mentor should be someone who's done that. That person will know the ropes and which direction to push you in.

FACING THE GIANTS

There's an inspiring scene from the movie *Facing the Giants* that I show to my students because it teaches a valuable lesson. It's come to be known as the death-crawl scene. A football coach challenges the team captain to crawl as far as he can down the football field while carrying a 140-pound player on his back.

The team captain says, "I can go about thirty yards."

The coach responds, "I want you to give me your absolute best."

Then the coach blindfolds the captain so he can't see how far he's crawled. By the end of the drill, the team captain who thought he could crawl only thirty yards made it one hundred yards, all the way into the end zone. The scene is inspiring because it proves that our limitations are often self-imposed. I suggest you take a few minutes to watch the death-crawl scene. You can find it on YouTube.

THE DIFFERENCE BETWEEN SUCCESS AND FAILURE

The value of having a good mentor in your corner and a massive belief in yourself cannot be overstated. It is the difference between success and failure, between achieving your dreams and watching them slip away. I have lived this lesson throughout my life.

When I have been without a mentor and lacked a massive belief in myself, I struggled. But with a mentor and a beast-type mindset, I got back on the path to success every time. The correlation is direct and profound, and it's why I teach all my real estate students to seek out and find a mentor. They are worth their weight in gold.

After my father passed, I didn't find another mentor until I reached adulthood. Just as my father had put me on the top of my game in baseball, this new mentor did the same, this time in real estate investing. He also taught me the power of my mind and of my resolve within. I value those lessons and principles about the power deep within myself more than any other lessons I have learned. They are the reason for my massive success today.

MY ADULT MENTOR

Fast forward a few decades. I had built a multimillion-dollar technology business and then watched helplessly as the dot-com bubble burst and took my business with it. I'll tell you that story in the next chapter. In a matter of months, I went from successful and on top of the world to broke, depressed, deeply in debt, and worried about my future.

Watching a business you built with your own hands decline and die is brutal. I had lost millions of dollars. I had mortgaged my house to the hilt and wasn't far from being homeless. I was an emotional wreck.

I isolated myself. I didn't want to talk to anyone. I refused offers of help, and I withdrew big-time. I adopted a me-against-the-world mentality, and the world was beating my ass.

That's when the universe brought me a great gift: a new mentor who would lift me up and out of the cesspool of self-pity and fear I was stuck in. I'll tell the full story in chapter 4, but for now, I just want to illustrate how critical this mentor was in my resurrection.

He saved me, and he did it with a healthy dose of tough love. There I was, feeling sorry for myself, without seeing the bigger picture. My mentor held my feet to the fire and gave me a much-needed perspective I had lost sight of. He taught me about my biggest asset: my mind!

HE TAUGHT ME ABOUT MY BIGGEST ASSET: MY MIND!

SHAME ON YOU

In my first conversation with him as my mentor, he made me realize how lucky I am just to have my health, the love of my family, a home, and to live in the greatest country in the world.

He said, "I'm going to be honest with you, Nick. Shame on you. Just shame on you, man. There are people right now on their deathbed hoping for one more day with loved ones. There are people who haven't eaten in days, people who want kids but cannot have them, who wish they had a wife and kids by their side. They would trade places with you right now, no questions asked. They would be thrilled to have the opportunity you have. But instead, you wear your failure identity on your sleeve."

"YOU WEAR YOUR FAILURE IDENTITY ON YOUR SLEEVE."

At first, I was shocked. Then I became angry. Who was he to talk to me like that? My initial thought was, "Screw you!" Yeah, I have my health. I have a wonderful wife and family who love me. Sure, I have a roof over my head and plenty of food to eat. Yes, I live in a free country, the greatest nation on earth, the land of opportunity...

Wait a minute. He was 100 percent correct. What he said hit me like a ton of bricks. As bad as my situation was, as much pain as I was in, that was only my perspective at that moment in time. It was the perspective of someone who went from being a multimillionaire to being knocked on his ass and having to start over. So what? Big deal. I did it once, so I can do it again. If not, I'm still going to be OK!

"Nick," my mentor said, "before we can dig into the real estate investing, we need to dig further into your most valuable tool: your mind! If we can get your head right, the rest is just one real estate door at a time for you."

My mentor gave me the gift of perspective. He also taught me the valuable tool of pattern interruption, a skill I have mastered and now teach to all of my students. I'll elaborate on it in chapter 4.

PATTERN RESET

That mentorship lifted me out of the swamp of depression and put me back on my feet. It enabled me to get back on top as the president and CEO of a multimillion-dollar business, which I love and which helps other people achieve their dreams. None of that would have happened if I had not deliberately sought out a mentor. If I had remained in isolation, with my me-against-the-world give-up mentality, I absolutely would not be where I am today.

You will hear much more in chapter 3 about how I found my mentor, Cris, and why having a mentor helped me so much. Proactively finding a mentor and then engaging with that mentor is something I recommend for those who want to push themselves and grow. But you have to go out and find the right mentor for you; that person won't just show up in your life. You have to make it happen.

I will always remember how awful it feels when you're

down and out like that. It's terrifying. The natural tendency is to avoid other people, especially successful people because they make you feel worse.

But retreating into isolation is a damaging impulse. If you ever feel that desire, you must fight it. No matter where you are in your life or business, I urge you to always reach out, seek out, and embrace positive role models and mentors. If you truly want to succeed, surround yourself with smart, successful people who will encourage you and foster courageous, calculated risk-taking and a winning mentality.

Fear of failure is normal. It's natural. No one wants to work hard and then come up empty-handed. So if you are afraid to fail, know that you are not alone. Everyone on the planet worries about failing. Acknowledge it and accept that the fear is there. Then move past it, despite the fact that it's in the back of your mind. We'll discuss some strategies for overcoming and dealing with fear in the coming chapters.

All humans are wired with a fight-or-flight instinct. In the case of the fear of failure, you have no choice but to fight like a beast. The harder you fight, the less scary it looks. Each challenge in life is only as intimidating as what we make it. We either make fear this big, nasty, scary mountain, or we learn how to pull back the curtain like Dorothy and her friends did on the great Wizard of Oz and realize it's just not so big, not so bad, and not so impossible to overcome. What a great feeling it is when you do.

All successful mentors have faced down their own fears and demons. They have walked the walk. They can empathize with your worries. But they can also encourage you to defeat those fears so you can do what you need to do to succeed. In fact, most highly successful people have personal and professional stories littered with failures. The common denominator of their success is their ability to get back up and keep going—to never stop, to know and recognize fear and say, "Screw you!" and keep grinding.

Don't go it alone. Find a mentor. Let him or her coach you until you achieve your goals and the success you desire.

A NASCAR ANALOGY

In NASCAR, it is common to see two drivers who are teammates help each other win races. One of the ways this is done is by allowing one car to draft behind its teammate's car. This is sometimes called slipstreaming. By following closely behind the first car, the second car reduces wind resistance and saves gas, allowing fewer pit stops and increasing the odds of winning. In other words, the first car is clearing the way for the second car.

A mentor is like a teammate you can draft behind. They'll help you reduce your resistance, save your fuel, and guide you to the best path forward. That's one of the great things about a good mentor: they can help you accomplish more by expending less energy so you can achieve more wins.

The wonderful thing about mentorship is that it works both ways. When I was struggling, Cris picked me up, dusted me off, and put me back on my feet along the path to success. I am eternally grateful for that. Now it's my turn to pay it forward.

I currently mentor others, including many of my students in the Nick Vertucci Real Estate Academy and the National Real Estate Network. I also like mentoring people who have tremendous potential but have wandered off the right path. For example, a colleague of mine has a bright, talented young son who happened to be ten years old at the time of this story, the same age as me when I first started tasting how failure felt. He also has a stepdad who has molded him into a great young athlete.

They moved him up to be on a more advanced soccer team. But then the other kids were a couple of years older than him. He started experiencing failure. All of a sudden, he wasn't the star player, and it was hard on him because that's all he knew about success at the time.

Slowly, he regressed and rebelled. He wanted to quit soccer. His mom, one of my staff members, asked me if I could speak with him. Of course, I agreed immediately.

I met with him and told him my story. I told him about my

father passing away and how I stopped trying because I was afraid to fail. I explained how I went through exactly what he was going through and that I knew what it felt like. I explained the years of pain and told him he could avoid this pattern if he wanted to.

"You're scared to try, aren't you? Because if you try and fail, then you have failed. You hate how it feels don't you?"

His eyes welled up with tears because I was right. He may not have even realized it until that moment. When I was ten and experiencing the same thing, I had no conscious clue that was happening. Most of us, even as adults, don't realize it either, and it crushes our dreams and success.

I taught this young man how to turn negative thoughts into positive ones using pattern interruption (see chapter 4). I told him, "It's OK to be scared, but you have to push past the fear, and give 100 percent effort." I made him promise me that he wouldn't let fear get in his way and that the next game he would go balls-out to play the best game he could, no matter what anyone else thought. I also gave him some homework. I asked him to write out his pattern interrupt and to keep repeating it out loud and in his head. I also taught him how to see the goal he was going to score and his other successes on the field. I told him he had to see it. Then he had to believe it. He had to have a plan, which was his training, and finally, he had to do *it*.

SEE IT. BELIEVE IT. MAP IT. EXECUTE IT.

"I want those other kids to dread the sight of you coming," I said. "Go so hard you leave nothing on the table after!" I kept asking him, "Are you going to go all out? Are you going to go all out?" He kept saying yes, and I kept asking until I was convinced my message landed.

I taught him that even if it didn't work out, as long as he gave it 100 percent, that would be a victory. He would not have this lingering negative feeling about himself. I told him that no matter what the outcome, he would feel better about himself because he would know he gave it all up on the field. No regrets.

His next game after that mentoring session, he played like he never had before. He did everything I said. He was aggressive, he ran hard and tried with all his might, and he scored a goal. He was like a completely different kid on the field because he was no longer worrying about failure.

His coach said, "Who is that kid and what the hell happened since last week?"

I'll tell you what happened: I informed him of a simple

success principle, and then he made the decision to be great and win.

Life is a game of inches, and sometimes one change of mindset, one small nudge in the right direction, can change the course of a person's life. That's why I'm writing this book: to nudge readers in the right direction.

Unfortunately, after my father passed away, there was no one to sit me down and give me that same mentoring. Instead of bouncing back after my father's death, I suffered through many years of fear, failure, and pain. I missed out on many opportunities. Because I was afraid to fail, I didn't even try. If I can help others avoid the pain I went through, then I will.

FAILURE BUILDS CHARACTER

In my experience, if you take ten people who all graduate from the same college with the same degree, chances are that only one or two will become a big success. Why is that? They went to the same college, they took the same courses, they have essentially the same education, and they probably earned similar grades. What creates the difference between those who succeed and those who fail?

The answer is, they decided not to let fear of failure or laziness win. They made the decision to be great and to win.

Failure is necessary to succeed. Successful people are not always the smartest. They're not always the most connected. They're not always the most educated. The most successful people are the ones who push past failure, break through boundaries, overcome obstacles, and are willing to get right back up and try again. They understand that failure is nothing more than a temporary speed bump on the road to success.

FAILURE IS NOTHING MORE THAN A TEMPORARY SPEED BUMP ON THE ROAD TO SUCCESS.

I tell my students at my trainings that not all of them are going to be successful in real estate investing.

"I know that's difficult to hear, because that's not what you expect to hear in a course like this. But it's the truth."

Then I tell them the good news.

"You are the ones who will determine who in the group is going to succeed, because if you don't do the work and put in the effort, you won't come out on top."

My students appreciate the straight talk. Most people just want the truth, and they respect you when you give it to them. My training company is not based on fluff or on pure emotion like the industry is known for. We will discuss that in later chapters.

MY TRAINING COMPANY IS NOT BASED ON FLUFF OR ON PURE EMOTION LIKE THE INDUSTRY IS KNOWN FOR.

But if they're willing to do the hard part, follow my rules, not take short cuts, persist past obstacles, listen to their mentor, and grind it out, they have much better odds of winning. Luck has little to do with it. Part of that is surrounding yourself with people who are doing what you're doing at a higher level, who are smarter than you in that area, who are more successful than you, and who are richer than you.

In contrast, if you surround yourself with people who are broke or with people who don't want anyone else to be successful, because misery loves company, you're never going to achieve anything. Your bar is set too low.

We don't surround ourselves with better, smarter, richer people to be pompous or act like we are better than others. Never. We do it to raise our own game. We do it to reach higher, not lower. Ultimately, we do it to build ourselves up so we can reach down and pull others up to success too. Never lose sight of that. You see, when we are healthy financially and emotionally, we have more to offer others. When you come from a place of abundance, not from a place of poverty, you can give more back to others.

WHEN YOU COME FROM A PLACE OF ABUNDANCE, NOT FROM A PLACE OF POVERTY, YOU CAN GIVE MORE BACK TO OTHERS.

My students consider me their mentor. They receive a certain level of mentoring when they train with me in my courses. I have thousands of students now in our network, so I cannot personally mentor them all. I've developed and designed a massive network of support, which includes mentorship at the highest levels. But regardless of the level of support and the method of interaction, that mentoring is critical.

Consider Michael Jordan again. Six NBA championships. Season MVP five times. NBA scoring leader ten times. Two gold medals in the Olympics. Was he one of the greatest basketball players of all time simply because of his God-given gifts? Absolutely not. Did you know he was cut from his high school basketball team and went home and cried? There were plenty of naturally gifted athletes who never rose to his level of success.

Was Jordan just lucky? No, it was something else. He achieved the pinnacle of success because he had a great mentor, because he never gave up, and because he worked harder than everyone else. He pushed himself to be the best, he practiced harder than anyone, he was the first one on the court for practice and the last one off the court, he shot more free throws, he put in the work, he ground it out, and he always went full throttle, giving 100 percent in every practice. When game day came, he was ready. In a nutshell, he made the decision to be the greatest and put in the work that was needed to be the best and to win.

"I'VE MISSED MORE THAN NINE THOUSAND SHOTS IN MY CAREER. I'VE LOST ALMOST THREE HUNDRED GAMES. TWENTY-SIX TIMES I'VE BEEN TRUSTED TO TAKE THE GAME-WINNING SHOT AND MISSED. I'VE FAILED OVER AND OVER AND OVER AGAIN IN MY LIFE. AND THAT IS WHY I SUCCEED."

—MICHAEL JORDAN

Michael Jordan was willing to fail so that he could succeed and ultimately be the greatest. And that's what it takes to succeed in any endeavor, including real estate investing.

CHAPTER TWO

———

MONEY INTELLIGENCE

I'm a huge football fan. Mostly NFL, some college. My favorite team is the Chicago Bears. I follow my teams and the general happenings in the NFL. So a recent article in the *Wall Street Journal* caught my eye. The headline read, "One in Six NFL Players Goes Bankrupt within 12 Years of Retirement."

Wait, what?

Yup. A high percentage of million-dollar-a-year professional athletes wind up broke. Remember superstar football players Terrell Owens and Warren Sapp? Each of them made more than $60 million in their playing careers, but they both declared bankruptcy.

In 2009, *Sports Illustrated* published an article indicating that the number of financially insolvent former athletes is much, much higher than one in six. That report stated that 78 percent of NFL players and 60 percent of NBA players are either "bankrupt or broke" within just two years of retiring from the league.

Athletes in other pro sports have the same problem. A few years ago, NHL superstar Jack Johnson declared bankruptcy, which is pretty unbelievable, because in 2011, he signed a $30-million contract.

How is this possible? How can someone go from making a million-dollar salary to barely being able to pay the rent, especially because the average NFL player makes more money in six years than the average college graduate will make in a lifetime?

The answer is that they lack money intelligence.

Most of these athletes are young and inexperienced, and they come into a lot of money without having any training or life experience in personal finance. To combat this problem, the NFL recently began offering an NFL Finance Boot Camp to help players conserve their money. In the program, current players hear from past players who lost everything as well as from financial planners.

That's a good start, but I can tell you from my own experience, developing money intelligence takes more than just a one-day seminar. It takes a concerted effort over many years.

Much like those professional athletes, the first time I achieved success in my life, I blew it. I totally blew it. I lacked money intelligence.

So let me share my story with you. It's a cautionary tale. I hope by sharing it, I can help others avoid the same mistakes. I made millions, then lost it all because I lacked money intelligence.

I MADE MILLIONS, THEN LOST IT ALL BECAUSE I LACKED MONEY INTELLIGENCE.

ENTREPRENEURIAL SPIRIT

It's painful to look back on the poor financial decisions I made, but during all those difficult times, I had two important things going for me: I had an entrepreneurial spirit and a strong drive to succeed and make money.

My first entrepreneurial experience happened by accident. During high school, as many young people do, I attended backyard kegger parties. (If my three daughters are reading this, please skip this paragraph.) I would locate the most happening party and hunker down there with kegs of beer and my friends.

There was this one kid who would always organize keg parties, and he'd charge an admission fee at the door. I always found myself paying the two-dollar entry fee. I would grab that infamous red plastic drinking cup and fill it up with beer. I started noticing that at the peak of every party, not long after I showed up and paid the cover charge, the police would show up and shut it down. The party would be over.

This happened three or four times, and then—*bang*—it hit me: this dude is filling up his yard at two bucks a pop and then calling the cops himself. After the police shut down the party, he was left with a full keg of beer and a pocket full of money. At first, I wanted to knock him out, but then I realized, "Wow, what a great business plan," and I actually laughed about it.

I thought to myself, "OK, Nick, you have a bigger back-yard than this guy does. There is no reason why you can't duplicate this brilliant business plan; you can also make it even better and bigger." That's exactly what I did. This was my first run-in with the power of duplication.

THIS WAS MY FIRST RUN-IN WITH THE POWER OF DUPLICATION.

I was off to the races, organizing keg parties and then calling the cops myself, for the rest of my high school years. Each weekend, I had a pocket full of cash and full kegs of beer at my house. Unlike that other kid, I let the party guests hang around a bit longer before the bad news broke: "The cops are here!"

The funniest part of the story is that other kid and I have reconnected on Facebook and messaged each other about the old kegger party routine. We had a good laugh about it.

CONTROL YOUR TIME, AND YOU WILL CONTROL YOUR DESTINY

From an early age, I knew I wanted to work for myself and be my own boss. That's why I never had any real desire to go to college. I wanted to be an entrepreneur, and I didn't want to wait until after college to do it. Plus, I just knew deep down it wasn't my path. I think I knew instinctively that not everyone fits into the same box. Society wants to herd us into the direction it wants us to go. Sadly, that means many people never become who they really want to be, could be, or should be. Don't get me started on this subject.

Nevertheless, reluctantly, I enrolled in junior college even though I knew this was not going to advance my dreams of entrepreneurship. I gave in to what society said I should do. After a few months, I said, "No way, this is not for me," and I dropped out. I was smart enough for college; I just didn't have the desire to succeed there because deep down, I knew it wasn't for me.

I wanted more, and I wanted it faster. I wanted to be a business owner. Looking back on it, I believe I learned more in just my first year in business than I would have in four years of college. Actually, I know I did. I experienced things that are not taught in college. Let me be clear: Having a great education is commendable, and I respect that a lot. It just wasn't for me.

Around that time, needing to pay the bills, I started working for a local electronics store called Phil and Jim's. It was like a Best Buy store. I began as a stock boy, then I drove a truck delivering TVs and appliances. I was nineteen years old, and soon I developed a reputation as a hard worker.

When the store had an opening for a salesperson, I applied. There were fifty applicants applying for two coveted sales spots because the salespeople could make a lot of money. I got one of the spots, purely on instinct. I'll never forget an older guy named Dave Alexander who was doing the interviewing. Dave later told me that there was one particular answer I gave to an interview question that landed me the job.

He said, "Nick, let's say you are selling a dishwasher, and the biggest spiff is on the KitchenAid, but the customer says he has always preferred Whirlpool and feels that's what he wants. What do you do?"

It just came right out. I said, "Dave, always give the people what they want and sell the KitchenAid to the next customer."

He looked at me for a second and said, "Damn straight you do!" He shook my hand and said he'd let me know soon. And bang! Twenty years old and I beat out at least fifty others for the spot.

Selling came naturally to me. I was good at it because I understand a couple of important principles: Tell the truth and listen. Don't confuse the situation and lose the customer's confidence. Also, I had a tremendous work ethic. I worked nights and weekends because I knew the more time I spent on the sales floor, the more commission I would make. By the time I turned twenty-one years old, I was the top salesperson in the company. At my peak, I was making about $80,000 a year in commissions. That was a lot of money at twenty years old and in the 1980s.

Here's why I believe I was so successful in sales. I listened more than I talked. I tried to really understand the customer. When I spoke, I spoke with absolute certainty, which I believe is critical to success. You have to be confident in what you're talking about. You can't confuse people and give them ten different options because, then, no decision will be made. Again, always tell the truth!

I knew I didn't want to make a career out of selling TVs and appliances. Yes, I was making more money than anyone my age, but when I looked at the older sales guys at the store, in their fifties and still selling TVs and appliances, I decided it was not for me. Everyone thought I was nuts when I walked away. But remember, I wanted to live my life, not someone else's.

DECISION TIME

At age twenty-two in 1989, I had about $25,000 saved up from working at Phil and Jim's, and I was looking for a new opportunity. My cousin, who was a bit older, and a friend of his were starting a computer technology business. They needed an investor, so they approached me. They knew I had some cash, so they asked me to be the third partner in their new venture.

It wasn't an easy decision to leave a good job with solid income and take a chance, but I knew I wanted more. I made the decision to be an entrepreneur and build a company in which I was part owner.

I invested my entire savings of $25,000. Again, like I said, everyone thought I was nuts. My coworkers at Phil and Jim's couldn't believe I would leave such a high-paying job. My friends and family thought it was too risky to invest $25,000. But it felt right to me at the time, and I did it. I left a high-paying job for a risky startup venture with, at best, an uncertain future.

One of the key principles I believe necessary for success in business and life is determined decision making. You have to be able to make tough decisions based on the information you have at the time. You won't always make the right decision, but if you delay making a decision until you have perfect clarity and complete data, then you'll spend most of your time waiting in limbo between decisions. Making no decision is a decision.

MAKING NO DECISION IS A DECISION.

I believe that in order to accomplish more in life, you have to do things. You have to commit. You have to go for it. That means you must make decisions and not look back. You have to be willing to put yourself out there. You have to learn to feel it before you achieve it. Most people are reluctant to do this. They hesitate, and the moment of opportunity passes them by.

I made the decision to leave Phil and Jim's and to invest all my money in a startup. It turned out to be the right one.

MY FIRST COMPANY

The business I invested in was essentially a computer

chip brokerage. We were buying and selling computer components. The computer industry was growing fast at the time, and the dot-com boom was just beginning. It was an amazing time to be supplying computer chips.

We did this for about two years, and then the partners split up. I was on my own for two more years until, eventually, my cousin and I merged once again and worked together for many years. Then we began thinking bigger. "Right now, we're just selling computer parts and peripherals," we said. "What if we put all the parts together and sold a whole white-box computer? We could really grow."

What started as a small, one-man company with a single desk and two telephone lines selling white-box computers gradually grew into a full systems integrator. We were basically a miniature version of Dell computers. We were building computers, selling parts, and doing cabling, and we even had a service department.

The entire computer industry took off like a rocket ship. My company benefitted along with everyone else. After a few years, I had a 25,000-square-foot building, almost 100 employees, and nearly $40 million in annual revenue. It was a great success story.

I wasn't even a techie. I had no computer training, but I was great with people, and I was good at understanding customer needs. Plus, as the saying goes, a rising tide lifts all boats. From 1989 to 2000, the computer industry was growing by double digits. We were in the right place at the right time.

It was an amazing eleven-year run. We were making more money than we ever dreamed. I was on top of the world.

But underneath the outward success, there was a serious problem: I was spending the money as fast as it came in. Throughout this incredible journey of success and growth, I hadn't saved or invested any of the money I made.

I HAD A HIGH INCOME BUT NO MONEY INTELLIGENCE

I had built my technology business into a multimillion-dollar enterprise, and I had a high income. But as fast as I earned the money, I spent it. I didn't spend it on appreciating assets such as real estate, stocks and bonds, precious metals, income-producing investments, or other money-making ventures. Nope. Instead, I squandered it on nonsense. I bought stuff.

I bought a huge home (my only good decision), extravagant jewelry, expensive cars, luxury goods, designer clothing, fine wines and spirits, vacations, Cuban cigars, and just about any other form of conspicuous consumption I could think of. My wife and I each owned several cars. I had a brand-new Mercedes and a new Hummer. All the cars were financed, and all required big monthly payments. Plus insurance. Plus maintenance.

But that wasn't enough. If I saw another car I liked, I bought it. On credit. I once spent $200,000 on landscaping! I also bought expensive patio furniture, outdoor fireplaces, sound systems, and endless other stuff for the house... mostly on credit. I even spent $100,000 to put in a fancy cigar room. Who has time to smoke cigars when you're going broke! I had come from nothing, so it was irresistible to have things that, at one time, seemed unattainable.

WHO HAS TIME TO SMOKE CIGARS WHEN YOU'RE GOING BROKE!

The truth was, we were spending it as fast as we made it, and almost everything I bought went down in value. For example, I bought two expensive motorcycles that I later sold for twenty cents on the dollar when I was liquidating just to survive. Just one example of many.

HIDDEN COSTS ADD UP

Because I had never made that much money before, I didn't realize that there are many hidden costs to living a luxury lifestyle. For example, expensive homes come with really high taxes, insurance, and maintenance costs.

Same with exotic cars. And when you add a $100,000 cigar room onto your house, that makes your property taxes go up.

I also didn't realize that spending tens of thousands of dollars on outdoor furniture, fireplaces, and sound systems was money I would never get back. You can't sell the bricks from your outdoor fireplace to pay the mortgage or buy food.

Living this kind of high-end consumerist lifestyle is addicting. You become addicted to buying and owning things. It becomes habit. You stop questioning whether you should spend $10,000 on a watch and just do it without considering the consequences. Then, before you know it, your bank account is getting drained faster than you can fill it up.

Then one day, your accountant calls and says, "You're broke."

THEN ONE DAY, YOUR ACCOUNTANT CALLS AND SAYS, "YOU'RE BROKE."

THE STORM WAS COMING

I'm sure you can see the storm that was brewing. The cause of the storm was that I didn't understand how to keep and grow my money. I had no clue what I was doing with my income. I had no idea where my revenue was going or how fast the money was leaving.

All I understood was that I was making a lot of money and having a ball spending it. My attitude was, "Hey, as long as the money keeps rolling in, we can keep on spending." My lack of experience and money intelligence cost me dearly.

What I learned later is that if you make wise financial decisions, you can still have fun, and you can keep more of your money and save and invest for the future. Smart investments can create tax shelters and deductions that lower your tax bill. Wise purchases such as real estate, precious metals, art, and collectibles appreciate instead of depreciate, the way cars and boats do.

Unfortunately, I was blissfully unaware of these principles as I was happily living in luxury and spending every dollar that came in. The sick part was that because of a lack of life experience, and ultimately a lack of money intelligence, I didn't see it coming. When it hit, it hit like Mike Tyson, the heavyweight champ!

WHEN IT HIT, IT HIT LIKE MIKE TYSON, THE HEAVYWEIGHT CHAMP!

THE STORM HITS HARD

Then the computer industry cratered.

The dot-com crash of 2000 slammed the brakes on the entire computer industry. It hit device, peripheral, and white-box companies like mine hard. My company limped along for over a year, and then 9/11 happened. It was a one-two punch to the economy as a whole and was felt acutely by small computer tech companies like mine still reeling from the dot-com collapse. Technology companies were going out of business even quicker than they had started up.

No one was buying. The orders dried up. I had millions of dollars in inventory sitting in a warehouse. I had tremendous overhead, office rent, employee payroll and benefits, and a personal lifestyle that necessitated a lot of cash pumping through the system.

It was like speeding along the Pacific Coast Highway at one hundred miles per hour in a Ferrari, and then the car in front slams on the brakes. My company went from one hundred miles per hour to zero in a matter of months, and I was unprepared for the impact.

In the end, the company was failing. The bank took over whatever assets were left, and I eventually had to walk away empty-handed. After years of pouring my heart and soul into a venture that I was proud of, that I had my whole identity wrapped up in, I found myself broke and without a plan.

KNOCKED ON MY ASS

The years 2000 to 2004 were the most negative, toxic few years I could ever imagine. It was one of the lowest points of my life. I remember many times driving in my car on the way to the office trying to choke back emotions but failing to do so. Trying to save that business and pouring the last bit of my home equity into it was financially and emotionally killing me. It added to the list of foolish things I did along the way.

I added to the pain of my business failing and being taken from me by the bank by leveraging my home. In a desperate attempt to fend off the banks, I mortgaged our family home. The house was leveraged way beyond its actual value. Back then, banks would let you borrow more than your home was worth. Because I hadn't drawn a paycheck in eighteen months, that home equity money kept us afloat. But you can finance your life on debt for only so long before it's time to pay up. Throwing good money at a bad situation was a huge mistake. Let me say that again if you missed it—huge mistake!

I had a growing family to provide for—my wife, two daughters, and another one on the way. We had built up such a big lifestyle that when it all came crashing down, my ego was crushed. I was embarrassed. I was supposed to be the breadwinner, but there I was, borrowing money against the house just to buy Christmas presents for my girls.

WHEN IT ALL CAME CRASHING DOWN, MY EGO WAS CRUSHED. I WAS EMBARRASSED.

I remember celebrating Christmas with the family from 2000 through 2004, trying to put on a happy face like everything was OK. But inside, I was slowly dying. I was a zombie as I sat there, watching my kids open presents that I couldn't afford. I missed out on those times even though I was physically present. Another huge regret!

At the lowest point, I was more than $3 million in debt. I owed $1 million in home equity loans, plus the money my business owed the banks, plus my office lease, which I was personally on the hook for. On top of all that, I had racked up about $150,000 in high-interest credit card debt. I could barely make the minimum payments.

PARALYZED BY FEAR

I didn't see any way out. There was no light at the end of the tunnel. I was angry with myself for taking equity loans out on the house, jeopardizing my family's home, and then putting the money into my failing company. In retrospect, that was absolutely the wrong move. Again, like I said, I was taking out a personal loan and throwing good money after bad. Big mistake.

The fear was paralyzing. I couldn't sleep. I would lie awake at night gripped by crushing anxiety. You may know what I mean: It's the witching hour at around 3:00 a.m. when all the fears hit you. Would the bank take the house from us? Would we be out on the street? Would I be able to provide for my family? I don't have a college degree, so I had no more options. Would I ever find a job or start another company? How would I make this right?

The more negative I grew, the more depressed and hopeless I became. I lost all my drive. I lost my confidence. I couldn't make decisions, and I couldn't even think clearly. It was a death spiral.

I remember thinking—and thinking very seriously—that I would be worth more dead than alive for the good of my family. Not many people know that fact. Well, now they do.

I literally had those thoughts, and they scared me deeply. I sank into depression. I just went through the motions of life, and it was hell on my family. I was missing out on some of the most important years of my children's lives. I was physically there, but I was just a shell.

The worst part of it was the regret. How had I built a successful company, made millions of dollars, and not saved or invested any of it? How had I gone from a cocky, self-confident, successful entrepreneur in his twenties, full of piss and vinegar, to a broke, paralyzed-with-fear, middle-aged man?

Every financial mistake I made played over and over in my head, haunting me. Later in the book, you will see when I had another opportunity at success. I vowed that I would never go through this again; I would learn from my mistakes. I would learn to build a business that could survive fluctuations and market crashes. I would focus on passive income that generated revenue, whether I was able to work or not.

I never wanted to feel this way again. I never wanted to live in fear again. I promised if I ever got back on top, I would help other people avoid what I was going through.

I NEVER WANTED TO FEEL THIS WAY AGAIN. I NEVER WANTED TO LIVE IN FEAR AGAIN. I PROMISED IF I EVER GET BACK ON TOP, I WOULD HELP OTHER PEOPLE AVOID WHAT I WAS GOING THROUGH.

WISDOM WAS EARNED, NOT LEARNED

Today, I look back and shake my head at all the financial

mistakes I made. Back then, I wanted lots of stuff and was willing to go into debt for it. I spent my money on depreciating assets and useless things that soon became worthless. Unfortunately, sometimes you have to earn that wisdom, and oftentimes, we reject the warnings until it's too late.

If only I knew then what I know now. Today, I know what's important and what is truly valuable. It's not owning a bunch of stuff. What's important to me today is providing financial security for my family and for the future.

My life is different now. I value peace of mind and financial security through passive income and real estate. That means I buy appreciating assets and investments.

For example, today I own millions of dollars of appreciating passive income properties. It is a powerful feeling to be set financially with massive mailbox money and passive income. Yes, I still have fun, and I have nice things. But the difference is that now I can truly afford them. I still use leverage as a real estate investor, but I won't overleverage for personal things, and I won't leverage at all for a depreciating asset. I can either afford to buy it with cash, or—no dice—I won't buy it. But with real estate investing and with educating myself, I will leverage all day long.

IT IS A POWERFUL FEELING TO BE SET FINANCIALLY WITH MASSIVE MAILBOX MONEY AND PASSIVE INCOME.

The difference between my life back then and my life now comes down to two words: *money intelligence.* I have it now; I didn't back then. I can only imagine where I'd be today financially if I'd had solid money intelligence twenty years ago. Most of the time, wisdom comes by trial or from a good mentor.

ACTIVE VERSUS PASSIVE INCOME

An important distinction is that my income from the technology company was active income, not passive income. In other words, I had to work for it and keep working to keep the money flowing. As long as I worked hard and sold lots of computers, the money rolled in. As long as the market was good, my income was good. But if I stopped working, the company went under, or the market tanked, my income would stop.

By relying solely on active income—money made from my direct efforts—I had put myself and my family at financial risk. Contrast that to passive income from investments and rental property, which continues whether you show up to work or not.

Back then, I didn't understand the need to invest in sources of passive income. I thought money was to be spent on cars and cigars, not saved and invested in opportunities that would in turn create more income.

But rainy days always come, sooner or later. At the time, I just saw the money coming in, so I thought it would always come in. I didn't understand that nothing lasts forever. So I never saw the point in saving or investing. When the rain came, it hit me hard.

WHEN THE RAIN CAME, IT HIT ME HARD.

WHAT IS MONEY INTELLIGENCE?

My lack of understanding money put me and my family in a vulnerable position. I had created a high-end luxury lifestyle that was built on the absolute necessity for the music to keep playing. If the music stopped, my world would crumble.

By going through such gut-wrenching times and watching my financial security destroyed, I learned my lesson. I learned to never again put myself or my family in such a precarious position. I learned not to rely solely on active income and instead seek out passive income opportunities. I learned to save and invest. I learned to pay off all my debts in full on the way up, when the money is rolling in, so when the music stopped, I wouldn't be buried in IOUs.

I learned that nothing lasts forever, not the boom times and not the lean times.

Perhaps the most valuable lesson I learned was the need for developing money intelligence. Just like those NFL players, you need to educate yourself on personal finance and money management. There are many ways to do this. Read books, take seminars, listen to podcasts, watch YouTube, and find a financial coach or mentor. More than anything, just be aware of it. I learned the hard way, but hopefully you don't have to.

I suggest you try all of those things. Make developing money intelligence a habit, even a hobby. It literally could be the difference between your becoming a millionaire or ending up flat broke.

Without developing a strong sense of money intelligence, most people will end up just grinding it out their whole life, working forty hours a week for active income. In other words, working a job for someone else. For many people, that's fine. Most people are hardwired to just work at a job and settle for a salary until they retire. In my experience, these are the type of people who spend more time researching and planning their vacation to Mexico than they do planning their financial future. I do not recommend this strategy or philosophy.

Just to be clear, working hard at a job is commendable; I do not look down on that at all. My point is that some of the people who are doing that want more, and I am saying there is more out there. It's right on the other side of fear. You should hop over that wall and enjoy some of it yourself.

IT'S RIGHT ON THE OTHER SIDE OF FEAR. YOU SHOULD HOP OVER THAT WALL AND ENJOY SOME OF IT YOURSELF.

IS $250,000 A LOT OF MONEY?

An important part of money intelligence is perspective. For example, when I am speaking to students from stage, I always ask my students this question: "Is $250,000 a lot of money?" I ask them to raise their hands if they think $250,000 is a lot of money. Like clockwork, almost every hand in the room goes up.

Then I say, "Keep your hand up if you think you could live off that amount of money for the rest of your life." There's a moment of hesitation, then almost every hand comes back down. With just a few seconds of thought, most people understand that $250,000 in the bank is not enough to live on.

In an absolute sense, yes, $250,000 is a lot of money. But as you grow your money intelligence, you'll realize that, invested conservatively, $250,000 will generate only about $18,000 a year in income (that's if your 401(k) doesn't become a 201(k) again if the stock market tanks), and that's being generous. So in a relative sense, $250,000 is not life-changing money.

THE CRASH WAS AN INSIDE JOB

If you want to understand why millions of Americans watched their 401(k) become a 201(k) in the 2008 crash, watch the movie *Inside Job*. You will be ticked off, but you'll see a small glimpse as to why it happened. You will understand why I buy brick and mortar and not paper.

What really is a lot of money? I always encourage my students to up their aspirations. I want them to think big. I want them to aim for life-changing money. Seven-figure money.

Think about this: $1,000,000 invested and earning a return of 7.5 percent will generate $75,000 per year in income. Now, for many people, $75,000 per year in passive income is enough to live off for life. But what about $2 million? Or $5 million? Or $25 million? The first step in making seven-figure decisions is thinking big and believing you can achieve seven-figure results.

I'll explain the origin of the phrase "seven-figure decision" and why I chose it as the title a little bit later in the book. All of business—and life—is a series of seven-figure decisions, but I want you to understand the profound moment when I figured that out. It's a story you won't even believe, but it's all true. So stand by and wait for it.

THE FOUNDATION OF MONEY INTELLIGENCE

The foundation of smart personal finance, which holds up everything else, is one simple principle: you cannot live above your means.

If you go into debt to live a certain lifestyle you can't afford, you'll be in poor financial shape for the rest of your life. The vast majority of Americans do this. They don't have the discipline to invest and save every month to pay cash for that bass boat, so they buy it on credit. Now, instead of investing and saving, they borrow the money for the boat and are paying interest on borrowed money. Someone once said, "Paying interest is the cost of being poor." The more things you buy on credit, the poorer you'll be. You have to invest and save, and if you live above your means, you cannot save.

"PAYING INTEREST IS THE COST OF BEING POOR."

Let's be very clear here: I am a professional real estate investor, and I believe in leveraging and paying interest...

under the right circumstances. I will even pay high interest for short-term money if it makes sense. It's second nature for me. But that interest I am paying must have huge rewards at the end of the investment. There is a big difference between borrowing money to invest and paying interest for a car loan or a boat that you can't afford and will depreciate to boot.

I also believe in education. I will invest in my future; you will hear more about this in later chapters. There is a huge difference between good debt and bad debt, and you never want to get them mixed up. I invested money in my real estate investing education. It was money I didn't have at the worst financial time of my life. But the result was that it changed the financial trajectory of my life forever. Again, wait for it in later chapters.

I INVESTED MONEY IN MY REAL ESTATE INVESTING EDUCATION. IT WAS MONEY I DIDN'T HAVE AT THE WORST FINANCIAL TIME OF MY LIFE. BUT THE RESULT WAS THAT IT CHANGED THE FINANCIAL TRAJECTORY OF MY LIFE FOREVER.

MONEY AND POWER IN AMERICA

The American financial system was designed for you to be in debt. I will have to be careful not to get political on this subject. But one of my passions now is understanding how things work in America and globally. All I'll say here is that you should educate yourself on how money and power works in the United States. Do a YouTube search on the Federal Reserve, quantitative easing, and fractional banking, and enjoy the bizarre ride of information you may not know.

STRATEGIZE A FINANCIAL PLAN

If you want to be financially stable and financially independent someday, you must have a financial plan. That plan should be guided by knowledge. If you go through life without a financial plan, without understanding budgets, investing, and compounding, then the odds are against you.

When you educate yourself, take courses and training, read books, listen to podcasts, and find the right mentors, you will develop confidence in your ability to make wise investment decisions. I teach my students how to invest in real estate. I arm them with the information they'll need to make shrewd real estate investment choices.

You should always know what you're doing when you decide to put your money somewhere. Have a plan, map it out, and make sure you're ahead of the game. The revenue that real estate investing can generate is a great source of passive income, also known as mailbox money. But you have to invest in yourself to build the money intelligence to know what you're doing.

TOP MONEY MISTAKES PEOPLE MAKE

1. Not investing their money and making it grow.
2. Not making saving a habit.
3. Spending more money than you make or living beyond your means.
4. Taking on too much debt for depreciating assets. There is good debt, such as investing, education, and real estate or other appreciating assets—never avoid those.
5. Not working within a budget, having no financial plan.
6. Excessive or frivolous spending.
7. Investments not diversified.
8. Buying depreciating assets: new cars, designer clothes, boats.
9. Overspending when buying a personal residence.
10. Investing without researching or having the right training and knowledge.
11. Always buying the newest and best (unless you can afford to pay cash).
12. And worst of all, not willing to invest financially in your own future.

I LEARNED THE HARD WAY

There are often two ways to do something: the hard way and the easy way. I gained my money intelligence the hard way, by making mistakes that cost me and my family dearly. I lost everything I had in order to learn about money. But you don't have to; you can learn the easy way.

I failed to invest the time in learning about money. I didn't make the effort to understand what to do with my high income. I didn't make a financial plan for the future because I didn't think I needed a plan. I was naive and didn't see the end coming. I didn't have a strategy in place for when my earnings dropped off a cliff. What was the result of that failure to develop my money intelligence? I had to learn the hard way and eat dirt.

Part of the reason I'm writing this book is to prevent other people from going through the disaster I went through. In this book, I'm urging you to build up your money intelligence. Find proper training. Learn how to save and budget and invest in real estate. If I had money intelligence back then, it would have saved me and my family a world of pain, fear, and worry.

As hard as it was at the time, I'm grateful for everything I went through. Even though I learned about money the hard way, at least I learned. Some people never do. Too many people go through their entire lives without money intelligence, and it costs them dearly.

When I walk into a big-box store and see a cashier or salesperson in his or her late sixties who still has to work to make ends meet, I think to myself that this is probably a person who never bothered to learn money intelligence. This is probably a person who never took any calculated risks or invested in their future. Hell, it could have been me if I didn't step out and if I had listened to the naysayers who told me not to quit that secure job I had when I was twenty-two. Guess what? The store Phil and Jim's is long out of business too. Get the message? Sure, there could be many reasons senior citizens choose to work late into their golden years, but one of them certainly is a lack of money intelligence. Again, there is nothing wrong with hard work, especially blue-collar work. It's the foundation of our country. But why settle for less if you want and deserve more.

BUT WHY SETTLE FOR LESS IF YOU WANT AND DESERVE MORE.

No matter what your income level is, whether you're a truck driver or a short-order cook, over a forty-five-year career in the old days, you could save enough money to retire without worry. But you need money intelligence to make that happen. In this new challenging economy, you must invest your way there now as well. Your money needs to grow and compound.

YOUR MONEY NEEDS TO GROW AND COMPOUND.

One of the best things you can do for your own financial future is to start using some of the resources available to begin to build your money intelligence. Don't settle for learning it the hard way like I did. It's no fun.

My first big success was the technology company, but I botched it. I lost everything. The second time around was a different story. The second time I became successful, I made much better financial decisions. I'm living proof that you can go from rags to riches, back to rags, and then back to riches. I can tell you that riches are better.

The second time I became successful, I immediately began investing my money in real estate. I started buying rental properties. I invested in assets that would produce positive cash flow and passive income.

LEVERAGE, LEVERAGE, LEVERAGE

As I have mentioned, be careful with leverage: it can be a blessing and a curse. I am a professional real estate investor, so of course I will use leverage to invest in real estate assets. I have borrowed millions of dollars to buy and sell real estate and to finance deals. But if I use leverage, I always have an exit strategy in place, even if it's a long-term exit.

Using other people's money (OPM) is a powerful tool. Sources of OPM include banks, hard money lenders, private money lenders, and so on. Do not leverage for stupid stuff such as cars and boats, unless you really can afford it if the note gets called.

Leverage is great when the economy is humming along and business is good. But when the market slows, interest rates go up, or buyers stop buying for whatever reason, that's trouble. If you're highly leveraged, you may not survive the downturn. If you avoid debt, you'll weather the storm much better. Basically, your leverage has to be able to survive the hard times as well.

Today, I try to keep debt to an absolute minimum unless it's good debt. Good debt is used to finance the purchase of appreciating assets such as real estate and education, which is invaluable. I strive for positive cash flow and passive income. If the economy crashed tomorrow or if I became sick or couldn't work, I wouldn't like it, but I could sleep easy and know that I would be fine. My family would be taken care of. We could live off just our large passive income and assets. There would be no banks knocking on my door demanding payment.

BUY FEAR, SELL GREED

The great investor Warren Buffett said, "Be fearful when others are greedy, and greedy when others are fearful." In other words, buy fear and sell greed. This basically means that smart investors often are contrarian to what the rest of the marketplace is doing. Most people follow the herd. If everyone is buying, the herd will follow the crowd and buy. That behavior is fueled by greed. "My neighbor made money buying tech stocks, so I'm going to do the same." That's when wise investors will sell, not buy, because it probably signals a bubble in the market. Likewise, when the herd is in a panic and trying to sell, that's the time to buy. Right now, as I am writing this, Bitcoin is the perfect example of herd mentality. Lots of money has been made, but I promise you, lots more will be lost when the bubble bursts. Just watch and see.

We all remember how the mortgage crisis of 2008 led to a huge recession. Let's look at what happened.

When the market was sizzling prior the bubble burst of 2008, everyone was making money—new home buyers, investors, mortgage brokers, appraisers, and anyone near or around real estate. They were all making truckloads of money. But here was the issue: it was fueled by greed, and almost everyone was just following the herd right off the cliff.

Most of the buying happened right at the top of the bubble

in 2008–2009. The media is always behind on the trends (and the truth) and was fueling the hysteria. The savvy investors knew this was an issue, and they were selling to the greedy at this time. The uneducated investors were buying, buying, buying. Then, of course, like anything that goes way up—*boom!*—it came tumbling down fast and hard. All the uneducated speculators got crushed.

OF COURSE, LIKE ANYTHING THAT GOES WAY UP— BOOM!—IT CAME TUMBLING DOWN FAST AND HARD. ALL THE UNEDUCATED SPECULATORS GOT CRUSHED.

From 2008 through 2013, I made more money than I ever have before in my life. Why? Because when everyone else was selling, selling, selling, I was buying, buying, buying. This was the time to buy, not before the bubble. Let's be clear: You could buy before the bubble, but you had to know what you were doing. You had to know that you were speculating, identify what the risks were, and understand the timing.

The markets were gripped with fear, and the media was now hitting that hard. Everyone was running away from real estate as fast as they could, even though now was the time to run toward it. Single-family homes—three-bedroom, two-bathroom houses—in areas such as Las Vegas and Orlando that had skyrocketed up to $300,000 before the crash were, at the low point of the market, being purchased for $40,000 or $50,000 at auction.

To take advantage of buying opportunities in down markets, you have to avoid common money mistakes. If you develop money intelligence, you'll have the liquid cash to invest in the great opportunities that down markets provide. If you're mired in unwanted, nonappreciating debt, you'll miss those opportunities. If you are educated properly in investing, you don't need money to invest in real estate. Well, let's be clear, you don't need your own money.

Don't worry if you do not have liquid cash right now. Most people don't have tens of thousands of dollars sitting in the bank. Neither did I. I know what it's like to start from scratch with nothing. I personally raised millions of dollars of OPM to do this, to buy, rehab, rent, and ultimately sell properties. I started with no money in the bank, and you can too. There are plenty of cash-rich investors out there who want to put their money to work in real estate, and if you do the work to find the investments, you can find the money. I was able to raise the OPM by finding networks of real estate investors, plugging myself into them, networking with them, and offering investments secured by the real estate assets. Just know that you can do this even if you don't have liquid capital, but you do have to get the training to develop the knowledge and then put in the effort to find good investments. Good investments will always attract money.

The main point of this chapter is that you absolutely must develop money intelligence. You can do it the hard way by getting wiped out, like I did. Or you can do it the easy way, by diligently learning about personal finance, saving, investing, and my favorite, real estate. If you're going to invest, you need to learn to do it right.

IF YOU'RE GOING TO INVEST, YOU NEED TO LEARN TO DO IT RIGHT.

TRUST BUT VERIFY

President Ronald Reagan coined that phrase when he was negotiating nuclear disarmament with the Russians. It's a powerful phrase I tell my real estate students. It's OK to trust people who want you to invest with them, but you have to do your due diligence. Don't just take an investor packet from someone who wants to do a joint venture with you and accept all their stated numbers at face value.

You need to research and understand the comps, or comparable properties. You need to understand the value of a property after it's rehabbed. You need to understand all the costs. You need to understand the business model. You need to understand the investment opportunity as well or better than the person who is pitching it to you. You need to know the rehab process better than your construction people, and the local market better than your real estate agents. You need to know every moving part.

You can still use those people on your team to accomplish things for you, but you can't just invest blindly. If you do, you're taking a big risk. You may win; you may lose. Trust but verify is always the only way to go.

FINANCIAL PLANNING

I always suggest learning about investing yourself instead of outsourcing it to a financial planner. You need to know what you're doing and understand how to analyze an opportunity. Of course, sometimes it makes sense to bring in a professional, such as a licensed financial planner or investment adviser. These professionals work with investing every day as their full-time job, so they have a solid knowledge base and, hopefully, a ton of experience. There is a lot they can offer. But that doesn't mean you don't have to know what you're doing.

I must caution you: Many financial planners and investment advisers have an agenda. Their goals may not be perfectly aligned with yours. For example, many financial advisers will discourage their clients from buying real estate investment properties. I never understood this. I built my fortune in real estate. But then I realized that investment advisers often earn commissions when they convince a client to buy stocks, bonds, or mutual funds. Of course, they try to steer their clients to invest in those types of securities instead of real estate. Some simply may have zero clue about real estate investing. They probably mean well, but they can hurt you by detouring you from, in my opinion, the best way to acquire wealth.

I believe that most financial planners, stock brokers, and investment advisers are honest, intelligent professionals with integrity. I'm not trying to discourage you from using one. I'm just saying that you need to be aware that their motivations and objectives may or may not be perfectly aligned with yours. When you receive professional financial advice, it may well be sound, but it may also be self-serving. As always, do your research, and trust but verify.

AS ALWAYS, DO YOUR RESEARCH, AND TRUST BUT VERIFY.

As I said above, I have found many financial advisers do not recommend buying real estate investment property because they simply don't understand it. Investing in real estate is a learned skill. Most colleges and business schools don't teach the nuts and bolts of real estate investing. So many financial advisers have not been properly trained in it. That's why it's not uncommon for a CPA or financial planner to advise one of my students not to spend money on taking my training courses.

It's unfortunate that they would try to encourage their clients not to educate themselves. I suppose an uneducated client would then rely more on the CPA or financial adviser, which works out well for them.

You know where I stand on this. The more we learn, the more we educate ourselves, and the more we build money intelligence, the quicker we will become financially independent. So I tend to question the motives of anyone who advises a client not to educate themselves.

THE MORE WE LEARN, THE MORE WE EDUCATE OURSELVES, AND THE MORE WE BUILD MONEY INTELLIGENCE, THE QUICKER WE WILL BECOME FINANCIALLY INDEPENDENT.

It's a real shame too because real estate represents one of the greatest financial opportunities for investors of all shapes and sizes. I've seen thousands of people with limited means and no education make money in real estate. Yet too many people avoid it simply because they don't understand how it works.

I tell my students that if they're going to learn, they have to pay one way or the other. They can either pay to take my education that provides high-end training and mentorship and learn from people who have done what they want to do, or they can pay by making costly mistakes on the ground in the market and losing a lot of money. Pay it in class, or pay it out in the field—you can decide. The latter is much more expensive.

Either way will provide valuable lessons and an education. But one way is much easier, less risky, less expensive, and more reliable. No matter what you do, there will be a learning curve. The question is, what's the easiest and most efficient way to climb up that curve? Do you want to learn from the school of hard knocks, by putting your savings at risk? Or do you want to learn from someone who's already accomplished what you're trying to do? I recommend applying that thinking and strategy to any new endeavor, not just real estate investing.

WHY BRICK-AND-MORTAR REAL ESTATE?

When I lost everything, there was one bright spot, one thing that saved me from completely going under and never recovering: my house. Yes, real estate. The only piece of real estate I owned at the time pulled my ass out of the fire and saved me from ruin. Let me explain.

After watching my technology business go boom and then bust, and after buying fancy cars, jewelry, and furniture, only my real estate kept its value. It actually kept appreciating in value. It was the only truly sound, long-term investment I had. I bought the house only because my wife pressured me into it. True story.

As I mentioned earlier, my wife forced me to buy the home in 1998. We paid about $500,000 for it. Today, it's worth closer to $1.8 million. Trust me, this lesson was not lost on me. I witnessed real estate's potential for appreciation in a dramatic way. It was the one stable asset I owned during all the financial turmoil and crisis.

I thought a lot about how remarkable that was. My world was burning to the ground, yet my house was solid as a rock. "Real estate," I thought, "that's something I want more of."

INVESTING IN REAL ESTATE (A CALL TO ACTION)

Investing in real estate is an excellent vehicle for accumulating wealth and achieving financial success. It's open and accessible to people of all ages, abilities, and incomes. But to do it safely and profitably requires a base of knowledge before investing. If you'd like to learn more, please visit http://nvrealestateacademy.com.

CHAPTER THREE

——

LIFE IS A GAME OF INCHES

In 2004, almost four years into slowly losing my business, I was barely holding on. Already in forbearance with the bank, I was a deeply depressed zombie on the way to work every single Monday morning. I was in my absolute worst emotional state ever. The only asset I had was a little bit of equity in my home. Banks at that time foolishly let homeowners strip their equity, so it was one thing I could fall back on just to survive.

YOU PAID $6,000 FOR A REAL ESTATE COURSE?

One day in the midst of my misery, I received a call from an acquaintance named Walt, a business owner who had built up the same kind of reckless lifestyle that I had, maybe worse. He lived too large like I did, he had no money intelligence, and he was overleveraged. He owned a packaging business, but he and I were in the same boat.

As they say, misery loves company, so we loved to share our bad news with each other.

On this particular day, he called to find out what I was doing on an upcoming weekend. It was a weekend in June 2004, and I had no plans, so he invited me to a three-day real estate class. He was planning to attend, and he was allowed to bring a partner.

"I thought of you," he said, "because we're both in the same boat and looking for some way to make money. Do you want to come with me?"

"Listen, Walt," I replied. "I need my weekends just to recover and recharge my battery enough to cry my way back in to work on Mondays. No, thanks. I'm not interested at all."

Then he told me something that blew my mind. He told me he'd paid $6,000 for the class. Six thousand dollars? For three days? It gave me a tiny bit of hope to learn that there was possibly someone dumber on the planet than I was. At the same time, however, once he put such a high value on it, I became intrigued.

LIFE IS A GAME OF INCHES AND DECISIONS.

But more importantly, the $6,000 put a value on it for

me, and ultimately—as you may already have guessed—I went to the event. Every time I tell that story or think of it, I get chills down my spine at the thought, "What if I didn't go?" It literally makes me shiver. As I type this right now, I'm experiencing that feeling. The reason is that decision changed my life and my financial trajectory forever. Life is a game of inches and decisions. I would not be here now, financially free, worth millions of dollars, and writing this book if I had not said yes.

By the second day of the class, I knew I was on to something. I called my wife, Gina, and said, "I don't know what I have here, but I'm starting to feel something. I don't know if it's hope. I don't know what it is, but I'm going to do something crazy. I'm about to spend a whole lot of money that we don't have." Remember, I was buried financially at the time.

The training was in Orlando, Florida, and was structured like a boot camp. Each day covered a different real estate strategy. On one of those days, the subject was cash flow properties. They taught us about buying rental properties and earning passive income. I had never understood passive income, and for the first time, I learned how it works.

It appealed to me because my computer business had been a constant active income treadmill. If I ever stopped running, the money would also stop. To make money in my computer business, I had to go buy the parts, assemble them, sell them, and collect payment. Then I had to repeat that process constantly in order to keep making money. When computers stopped selling, the well dried up.

I DEMANDED MENTORSHIP

The idea of passive income resonated with me because I wanted to build something that I didn't have to worry about, where a turn in the market wouldn't be the end of the money. Even though the process of building a passive income system is a long haul, I was enamored with it. I had stars in my eyes for the instructor of that boot camp, Cris, and I wanted to be just like him. I wanted what he had—financial freedom!

Being naive, not realizing how busy Cris was, and not realizing that he sees thousands of students and he's booked more solidly than anyone investing in real estate, I approached him and started asking him questions.

"I want more of this," I said. "How do I learn more?"

At first, he gave me the standard answer. "Just take what I taught you and put it to work."

"No, I need more than that," I replied. "Can you help me? Will you coach me?"

He said, "Look, I have thousands of students. Plus, I have a family, and on top of that, I'm investing all the time. But I'll give you my email address. Every once in a while, if you have a question, feel free to ask. I can't promise you that I'm going to be right there for you all the time."

Something inside of me wouldn't take no for an answer. "I understand, Cris," I said. "But would you give me a day or two? A couple of days, that's all." I realize now, looking back, that it was an absurd request. That's how desperate I was to learn about passive income. His response didn't surprise me.

"I can't. Sorry."

But I wouldn't take no for an answer. "OK, look, if you give me two or three days, I'll pay you $10,000 for one-on-one instruction. I just need to know more, to see how this works, to touch it. That's how I am. Even when I was in school, once I understood something, I understood it, but first I had to see it in action."

"Nick, I don't need the money," he said. "I can't do it. I have thousands of students, and I teach them during these sessions, and that's it. I couldn't give you three days even if I wanted to."

"OK," I replied. "What if I paid you $20,000? I don't have it, but I'll get it."

"I can't."

"OK, I'll tell you what," I said. "I will pay you $30,000 if you'll spend three days showing me how to make this work." Don't forget, I didn't have the money. I still had a little equity left in my home, and I knew I had to have this mentorship.

He smirked for a moment. I fully expected him to say no again. "OK, OK. When do you want to do this?"

I learned a valuable lesson that day. Everyone has their number, and I'd finally reached his. We got out our calendars and scheduled three days together so he could show me the ropes. It was a major turning point for me.

THE TRUTH BOMB

What I didn't realize during that period of my life was how I wore my failure identity on my sleeve. Everything that came out of my mouth was self-pity and woe. From the moment I first met Cris, I vomited all of my misery and fear onto him. I was scared, and I wanted a little bit of hope at any cost.

From the time I was young, my identity had been wrapped up in my achievements. I'd always been a successful entrepreneur. Everything I touched turned to gold. But

I'd become this incredibly negative person during my downward financial spiral.

My negativity was obvious, even to Cris. A few weeks later when we met for the three days of one-on-one coaching, Cris wanted to have a serious talk with me as we were getting started.

He sat me down and said, "Hey, Nick. Let's chat. Can I be really candid with you?"

"Of course. That's what I want."

"Fine. Let me ask you a few questions. Do you have any health problems that I don't know about? Are you terminally ill?"

"No, I'm healthy," I said.

"How about your wife and kids? Is there anything more important to you? Are they healthy?"

"Nothing is more important. They're perfectly healthy."

"Some people don't even have a wife and kids," Cris continued. "That's their life goal, to have a family. You already have that. Do they love you?"

"Yeah, like crazy."

"If you lose your house and you have to live in a small apartment, are they still going to love you?"

"Of course."

"Do you eat three meals a day? Do you and your family have enough to eat?"

"Always."

He gave me a stern look and said, "I'm going to shoot straight with you, Nick. You seem like a great guy. I know that you were successful at one time and that you've hit a rough patch. But from the day I met you, all you've talked about is how screwed you are. I'm not downplaying the magnitude of your reality or your feelings, but I have to say something. If it offends you, so be it."

I held my breath waiting to hear. What he said next stunned me.

"Nick, shame on you, man. Just shame on you. There are people lying in hospital beds right now on their last breath. They would give anything just to live another day. They would trade places with you right now even if it meant being buried financially. They would love to have the opportunities that you have. There are no guarantees in life, Nick. You wallow in your own self-pity and negativity. Why? Because you lost a lot of money. So what? You have every other gift in the world. Shame on you."

He reminded me that I have everything that is truly important in this life, everything that billions of people on this planet desperately want, yet I was wallowing in my own self-pity and self-created misery.

He continued, "Unless you change your identity, unless you stop feeling sorry for yourself, nobody is going to want to work with you. I'll teach you how to do that. I'll show you all I know, but nobody wants to work with a negative person. Honestly, you won't attract anything positive into your life with that attitude. I know you're screwed. I can feel it. It's a vibe dripping off you, and it's real. But you have to stop thinking that way. There are people sleeping in cardboard boxes, and you're here with me, and we're going to lunch afterward. So your life is not going the way you want it to, but how are you changing it with this negative attitude? You told me you're paralyzed with fear, you're depressed, but how does that fix anything? Knock it off, or you'll never be successful."

I was stunned. I went silent. What could I say? For a minute or two, I stood there and felt offended. But then it was like being jolted awake with jumper cables. It shocked me back into reality. In that moment, I knew the truth: Cris was absolutely right.

He began to tell me about pattern interruption. He taught me about the strength of the mind and shared with me the principles of successful people. Successful people, he said, aren't the smartest people in the room. If you put a group of the smartest people on that TV show *Jeopardy!*, one of them might become the next game show champ and win a million dollars. But many of the most brilliant people in the world don't turn their IQ into dollars. The truly successful people in life usually aren't geniuses, and they don't know everything. Instead, they have the right perspective, they work hard, and they maintain a positive attitude. Most importantly, they have the will to succeed at all costs. They will take the hits to get there. They will eat dirt on the way if that's what it takes. Their mind game is massive.

"Look, Nick, you've already built a business once," Cris said. "You're obviously someone who can do it. You've proven that. Now you have to realize and remember or maybe really learn the principles of success. You put yourself in even more good debt here because you're trying to accomplish something. All of the components for success are in place. You've just lost sight of them." He said, "You have the vehicle that can drive you where you want to go. That is real estate investing. Now you need to tap into your best asset and your strongest muscle—your mind."

"YOU HAVE THE VEHICLE THAT CAN DRIVE YOU WHERE YOU WANT TO GO. THAT IS REAL ESTATE INVESTING. NOW YOU NEED TO TAP INTO YOUR BEST ASSET AND YOUR STRONGEST MUSCLE—YOUR MIND."

THE TRUTH CHANGED MY LIFE

That conversation changed my life. The message penetrated my core, and Cris reinforced the lessons over the next three days by teaching me how to hold on to the right perspective. He taught me that developing the right mindset is the first step toward success. That's something I teach to my students now. I don't want them to come into my four-day bus tour event, get all pumped up, and then just leave, expecting everything to happen just because they're pumped up and excited. They need to know how to develop and maintain the right mindset—what I call mind game—over the long term. Of course, they also need the best real estate investing training to go with it. Remember, you need a sound success vehicle to go along with your strongest muscle, which is your mind. If you combine those two things, you won't be able to be stopped.

The truth is, most people don't reach their goal because they don't believe they can achieve it and because they don't get off their ass and work for it. You have to push through the fear every day if you want to win. I warn my students that they're going to forget some of the things I tell them when they leave my training event, so it's their responsibility to stay on track. If they don't do that, they'll fall back into their old patterns because that's human nature. They've spent more time in the old negative way of thinking, so it's too easy to go back to thinking and acting that way.

Unless you do the things you're supposed to do every single day and work on your mind game every single day, you won't make it, because the real battlefield is in your head. That's what I learned, and I never forgot it.

After my three days with Cris, every time I started feeling the old negativity creeping back in, I recognized it. I knew what it was, so I didn't wonder, "Why am I feeling this way? Shouldn't I feel better now?" I learned to expect it, and then I took hold of it and crushed it into pieces and moved on. No matter how often or frequent, I would catch it and repattern it and put myself back in the right mental place. I kept doing that, day after day, no matter how hard it was. Slowly but surely, by taking control of my thoughts, I gained confidence, I built momentum, and I started getting results.

TAKING ACTION ON WHAT I LEARNED

After my mentor helped me screw on my head straight, I began changing my mind game and taking action. I started to build my real estate business based on what I learned in my training and more specifically from Cris. To do that, I had to set specific daily goals, because I was still dealing with the disaster of my old business. I still had responsibilities with my wife and kids every day. The massive financial undertaking did not just disappear, but I did see it more clearly and started to believe I could do this.

In order to build my new business, I had to set goals and meet them with no excuses. I couldn't say, "Oh, I'm too busy today. I'll do this tomorrow." No, I had to physically put everything in motion because, again, you can believe in it all you want, but if you don't take action, nothing happens.

Every single day, I worked to build my real estate investing business, whether I felt like it or not, whether I felt like I was making progress or not, even if I was rejected all day long. I kept working at it religiously, and I kept my mind strong. Buying properties here and there, a little bit at a time, putting one foot in front of the other, I made progress day by day, and I slowly made it to where I am today. That's how it works: mix a strong mind game with a specific plan and then execute the plan. I was taught to invest and do one door at a time until one day you look back and see a ton of doors. (*Doors* is a real estate term for properties.)

FAILURES ARE OFTEN HIDDEN, BUT SUCCESS SPEAKS FOR ITSELF.

Not everyone who reads this book will have experienced a real, hard failure in life, but a lot of you have. The most successful people on the planet have failed more than they've succeeded, but you've only heard about their successes. Failures are often hidden, but success speaks for itself. What I am doing is exposing most of my failures for your benefit in hopes that it sends a message. Remember, just because you don't succeed in something, or something doesn't work, doesn't make you a failure. Sometimes it's just because it was your first try. I've had plenty of things that didn't work out. Despite all my failures and disappointments, I'm experiencing tremendous success now.

When I was losing my computer business, one of the most difficult things to deal with was my ego. I felt embarrassed that I was losing my company, embarrassed that I wasn't the top dog, embarrassed by what I'd failed at rather than proud of what I'd built.

In late 2013 and into 2014 when I was planning and launching my real estate training company, one of the biggest struggles I had was the fear that it wouldn't work, proving those people right who had scoffed at my business and said I was going to fail. If I failed at this, they could've pointed their fingers and said, "I told you so. We were right. You can't do this on your own." You will hear more about that in later chapters.

THE DEVIL WHISPERS, "YOU CAN'T WITHSTAND THE STORM."

THE WARRIOR REPLIES, "I AM THE FUCKING STORM!"

I decided not to let the fear stop me. Instead, I faced the storm. You may have heard this saying in the past. It's one of my favorites.

> The Devil whispers, "You can't withstand the storm."
> The warrior replies, "I am the fucking storm!"

I don't know about you, but that fires me up! You have to rid yourself of your shame and fear of failure even before you try something. If you failed in the past, fear may hinder you from trying again. Don't let it. If you don't try again, you'll never make it. Unfortunately, that's what I did when I was a kid: I stopped trying. I figured if I stopped trying, I wasn't failing anymore, and if I wasn't failing, then I didn't have to feel embarrassed. We go away from our pain instinctively. When you don't like a certain emotion, you head in the other direction. But now, all I know is, I am the fucking storm.

This is especially true for people who have alpha or type A personalities. If that's how you're wired, then you have to dump that shame and embarrassment right away. Sadly, millions of people won't even take a chance or make a calculated risk toward success because they don't want to risk embarrassment. Even if you fail, even if you don't make it, at least you tried. You did what most people won't do, which means you have more courage than they do, and you're much more likely to succeed.

Most people prefer the safety, security, and low risk of punching a clock. Either they're too lazy, too comfortable, or too afraid to go out there and grab the big opportunity by the balls and just go crush it. Be proud of yourself, just trying is half the battle. Even if you fail four times to finally succeed on the fifth try, it will be worth it a thousand times over. Bottom line: just be the storm!

NO HARD WORK, NO DICE

I always tell my students real estate is not a get-rich-quick scheme. If you want a get-rich-quick scheme, go buy a lottery ticket. But if you want a reliable way to make money, you have to go out there and work. You have to put in a lot of sweat equity before you experience results.

Even flipping your first house could take 120 to 180 days before you see any return. As soon as you get the return, you have to go flip the next one. You have to make the calls and put in the work every day. You have to work at it and keep grinding, even when you feel like you're not getting anywhere. It's hard work, and you have to put in the time. It's the only way success will come to you. In this business, it's one door at a time, then two doors, then three, then 840 in two years like I did. But waiting for it to happen won't work.

If you do that long enough, however, you build momentum. That's when you start seeing big money. For some people, it happens relatively quickly, but for others, it doesn't. If you don't see the big money for a while, don't start feeling like it will never happen. Don't give up and assume that you'll never achieve success or that it's simply not meant to be. That isn't the case.

Your perception that this would be easy is the problem. Maybe somebody told you it would be easy, so now you feel disappointed and discouraged and start making excuses. Remember, you're learning a trade that you can use for the rest of your life, but it's a business. It's something you have to work hard at. I tell my students, if you make one good deal, you'll earn the tuition back that you spent on your educational investment. That means the rest of the money you make is pure profit, and the potential return is infinite.

If you do just one flip this year and make $50,000, that's a $50,000 bonus for maybe ten to twenty hours of actual work. What if you did four of them? What if you made only $25,000 each, but you did six of them? What if you did 840 properties in two years like I did?

Start thinking of the business that way, and it'll start to work for you. Don't just pump yourself up on the idea that we're all going out there and becoming millionaires overnight. You can become a millionaire if you want to, but you have to work at it and put in the time.

The training I received initially by the educational company I went through wasn't good. A lot of their tactics simply didn't work in the real world. There was no support and no network. But my one-on-one mentorship training on cash flow and mindset was invaluable. The first couple of flips didn't change my situation at all, but I was determined, and I kept grinding away, one door at a time. Building positive cash flow took years, but it did happen. Dump the idea that success happens overnight; it rarely does.

DUMP THE IDEA THAT SUCCESS HAPPENS OVERNIGHT; IT RARELY DOES.

CHAPTER FOUR

PATTERN INTERRUPTION

One of the most important things my mentor Cris taught me during our three-day session was how to deal with fear. I had all of this pent-up anxiety because of my circumstances, and I was making it worse by being afraid. I was giving fear 100 percent dominance over me. As humans, we're wired to feel fear. It's a natural fight-or-flight instinct designed to keep us safe.

At the same time, fear is what you make of it. Fear can be controlled and managed. You decide what kind of monster it is, how big and how dangerous. Is it so small it's not even a factor, or is it going to grow so big that it dominates your life? That's up to you. Remember when they pulled back the curtain in *The Wizard of Oz* and realized that the reality was the great Oz was just one big hustle? Remember that reference for later in my story coming up.

Fear lies at the center of all of my negativity. Fear of losing my house, fear of looking stupid, fear of not being able to provide for my family. I had let it take over everything.

TURNING SELF-HELP INTO DOLLARS

I believe in self-help, but it can't be something you do only in your mind. In business, you need more than a strong mind; you need a solid financial vehicle. You can make all the changes to your mental and emotional state you want, but without a vehicle for that strong mental game, you won't make any financial impact. You need to take your positive mindset and put it into a solid financial vehicle, grab the wheel, and drive like a beast into success.

For me, the vehicle was real estate investing. A positive mindset alone won't make checks show up in the mail. You have to get off your ass, burn the midnight oil, and work harder than the next person. When you do that, the checks start showing up.

The mind is your strongest muscle and the source of your self-help. But you must combine it with a realistic vehicle that you can actually operate, then you start to accomplish great things. For example, I might dream of becoming an NBA basketball player, but it's never going to happen. No matter how badly I want it, no matter how hard I try or how much I practice, it's not the right vehicle for me. I will not be dunking on anyone anytime soon. I had to choose a realistic vehicle that I can actually operate. That's what I love about real estate investing: anyone can do it.

Sometimes self-help courses set people up for failure by not being realistic. The principles might be correct, but the mindset must be balanced with action. Everything's not always going to work out. Just because you visualize something doesn't mean it's going to happen. Just because you put some good principles into practice doesn't mean everything will change. The right mindset must be paired with the right actions, the right plan, and the right vehicle.

THE RIGHT MINDSET MUST BE PAIRED WITH THE RIGHT ACTIONS, THE RIGHT PLAN, AND THE RIGHT VEHICLE.

I HAD TO SHAKE THE POVERTY MENTALITY

When my computer business tanked, I became jealous and covetous. It hurt me to see other people in my social circle remaining successful while I went down in flames. That's a poverty mentality.

Jealousy creates a negative vibe that will only hurt you. Jealousy won't help you get what you want. It actually has the opposite effect.

In contrast, a wealth mentality sees another person's success and says, "Good for them. They've obviously worked for it. They've earned it, and it doesn't affect me one way or the other." A wealth mentality strives to learn from the success of others in order to achieve like they have.

TWO PEOPLE GO INTO A ROOM

Why obsess over the bad things? It takes so much of your energy. Why not put that energy into making your situation better instead of worrying about what's wrong in your life?

In my computer business, when things were bad, my cousin, who was also my business partner, and I would sit and complain all day long about how awful everything was. Instead of saying, "Let's start figuring out a solution," we just shared negativity. In that case, there was no solution. Our cheese was moved.

Even if there wasn't a solution, we still would have been better off pouring our energy into trying to find one. All we did was focus on the bad, and it made things worse.

There's an old parable about two people who go into a room. One of them is negative and the other is positive. A day later, they'll both come out of the room negative. That's just how negativity works. You have to stop negative thoughts before they start. This doesn't mean your problems aren't real or that you're burying your head in the sand and pretending everything is fine. It simply means you're controlling when and how you think about things.

WHAT IS PATTERN INTERRUPTION?

Pattern interruption means replacing negative thoughts with a different, new or better, and more positive pattern of thinking. For example, let's say you're having thoughts of, "I'll never be able to afford to own a home." If you let those thoughts go unchecked, pretty soon, you'll believe it. Instead, interrupt that pattern by replacing those thoughts with, "I'm going to be a homeowner within twelve months. Then I'm going to buy rental property." Then you just keep repeating that thought until it drowns out the negative thoughts. Try it and see how quickly pattern interruption makes you feel so much better.

You have to stay militant on this. Pattern interruption isn't something you do just once or twice. Make it a daily habit. Negative thoughts are going to continue to come back, so expect that. You have to stay vigilant.

Some people become caught up in negative patterns because of how they're wired. Negativity might come from fear or adverse life experiences. Sometimes people are just inherently negative, or they spend time with someone who is, and that negativity of thought becomes a persistent pattern.

You always want to hold positive thoughts in your mind. Positive people believe that good things will happen to them. They just know they're going to find that great parking spot. Negative people think, "I'll never find a parking spot. Forget it. I'm not even going to try. I'm going home." By not trying, they guarantee that they will not, in fact, find a parking spot. I know I am getting a parking spot now.

When we fall into a negative thought pattern, our minds can run away from us like a runaway truck on a steep downhill grade. If you start thinking negatively, one negative thought follows another, and pretty soon, your whole day looks like it's going to be a disaster. When it comes to your thoughts, you can feed the beast by just letting your mind go off on its own. You have to stop it and replace negative thoughts with positive ones. Luckily, it works the same way with positive thoughts. When you think positive thoughts, more positive thoughts will follow. When you add action, positive things will start happening. I am telling you, without a doubt, your thoughts and actions today will be your tomorrow. Good or bad. That statement you can take to the bank.

I AM TELLING YOU, WITHOUT A DOUBT, YOUR THOUGHTS AND ACTIONS TODAY WILL BE YOUR TOMORROW.

For me, pattern interruption helped me replace the fear that had taken control of my life during the loss of my tech business. My mentor Cris taught me to banish the negative thoughts that fed the fear, to replace them with positive thoughts, and then to reinforce those positive thoughts with repetition. The best way to reinforce a positive thought is by saying it, thinking it, saying it, and thinking it until it becomes part of your DNA.

Using pattern interruption pulled me out of depression. It helped me to realize that I could achieve anything I set my mind to. It can do the same for you.

HOW PATTERN INTERRUPTION WORKS

Here are the steps to pattern interruption. First, you have to recognize the need. You can identify the negative pattern asserting itself when you feel yourself drifting in a downward direction. Then interrupt those thoughts, replace them with positive thoughts, and turn your whole mindset and mood in a positive direction. Redirect your mind, control where it is going, and know why you're doing it. Have absolute certainty when doing so.

When I first learned this, I had to practice pattern interruption every few minutes. As the positive outlook took hold, I would need to pattern interrupt only every few hours. Each time the fear and anxiety tried to come back, I had to hit it hard with pattern interruption. The negative thoughts are sneaky, and they slipped up on me so easily. Anytime I wasn't focused on something positive, the negativity soon came back.

After a while, however, I started to change how I felt. When you interrupt the negative pattern enough times, you genuinely start to convince yourself that you're going to be OK no matter what. Because the reality is, you are going to be OK. It happens by degrees. You start by doing pattern interruption every minute, hour, then every few hours, if that's what it takes. Then you gain momentum, and it becomes a few times a day. How quickly that happens depends on how deeply rooted the negative pattern is. You have to keep at it as long as it takes. And always revert back to it when needed.

I always try to remember this. No matter how bad things seem, you're probably luckier than the next guy. You have a lot more going on than many people in the world. Start from there, rather than starting from a perspective of envy and coveting what someone else has. So what if my current business fails? Yes, it would suck. I wouldn't enjoy it, and many people are dependent on me. But the fact of the matter is, I've had a good run.

Even if it ended tomorrow, it would still have been a wild success. I did things most people haven't done. I still have enough money that I could live off for now. I would just play the next hand I was dealt. At this point, I am set for life most likely, but I am telling you that even if I wasn't, I wouldn't sweat it. I am too busy enjoying my current blessings. I'd deal with that if it came. I've learned not to miss out on life over worry.

I'VE LEARNED NOT TO MISS OUT ON LIFE OVER WORRY.

UP YOUR ASPIRATIONS AND LIMITATIONS

The expectations you place on yourself can come from many sources. They might be from your parents, or they could be the result of your siblings' accomplishments, or even from what people told you when you were a kid. Many things influence the way we view ourselves, what we think we're capable of, and how much we think we can achieve.

For me, when I was in school, I just knew college wouldn't be in my future. That thought lingered in the back of my mind since I was a boy. I didn't come from a long line of successful entrepreneurs or college graduates, so I didn't have that expectation either. My limitations, in some sense, were already set.

But I wanted more. I always believed I could achieve more. I knew I had some good qualities and talents that others lacked. What I learned over time is that you dictate your own limitations; it doesn't matter what other people have placed on you. If you want to, you can raise the bar, and that's what I try to do continually. I never rest on my past achievements; instead, I constantly challenge myself to reach for the next level. I take calculated risks, but I do it the right way, the safe way.

WEALTH MENTALITY

Sometimes people say to me, "If you're so damned successful, why are you showing other people how to do what you do?"

Yes, I'm successful, but I'm not worried about someone else going out there and scooping up all the foreclosures. A person with a wealth mentality shares information and helps others. If you truly want to achieve success, you surround yourself with people who are more successful than you because they inspire you to up your game.

A PERSON WITH A WEALTH MENTALITY SHARES INFORMATION AND HELPS OTHERS.

The more money you have, the more resources you have, and the more ability you have to help people and help the world. As Leonardo DiCaprio said in the movie *The Wolf of Wall Street*, "You can save the spotted owl with money." The idea that to really help humanity you should give away all your money until you're broke is complete nonsense.

I'm able to do so much more for people now because I'm financially strong. In fact, I help other people more than I help myself because I have the ability to do so. If I was struggling every day just to pay the bills, I wouldn't be able to think twice about helping anyone else.

IF I WAS STRUGGLING EVERY DAY JUST TO PAY THE BILLS, I WOULDN'T BE ABLE TO THINK TWICE ABOUT HELPING ANYONE ELSE.

PROTECT YOUR ENVIRONMENT FROM NEGATIVITY

After the training with my mentor, I started putting everything he'd taught me into play. I was still in the computer business at that point, but I stopped having those negative meetings with my business partner. It put a wall between us. He thought I was just sticking my head in the sand and refusing to deal with problems. When he tried to start those pessimistic conversations, I would tell him, "Look, I'm not participating in a negative thoughts session for two hours. I recognize the problem, but I'm not going to give it power, and I refuse to dwell on it and give it power. I won't put myself in a funk where

I can't function and do the things that could help us or help myself."

If he persisted in speaking negatively, I left the room. He didn't like that, and he didn't believe in self-help. Actually, he thought I was an idiot with all of this new positive attitude stuff, but I stuck to my guns. My partner was my cousin, and he is a smart and talented guy, so when I say this about him, understand that was just his style at the time. It was mine too, for a long time, so I cannot blame him. He's a great guy and was a good partner for many years. I was now on a different path and would not veer off it.

I have said this before and will say it again. If you put one positive person and one negative person in the same room for enough time, they will both come out negative. You have to protect your mind game. Again, I am not suggesting that just being positive will fix your issues, because it won't. You need that mindset to be strong so you can think clearly and go get your hustle on and grind it out.

YOU NEED THAT MINDSET TO BE STRONG SO YOU CAN THINK CLEARLY AND GO GET YOUR HUSTLE ON AND GRIND IT OUT.

Negativity is contagious. Humans are just wired that way. So control your environment. That's what I started doing.

The meetings with my cousin created a toxic mood, so I refused to feed into it. That caused a lot of tension with my business partnership. Everyone thought I was spiraling off into la-la land. They thought my attitude was unrealistic, but the opposite was true. I understood the problems we were having. They hadn't gone away, but I wouldn't let them dictate my life anymore.

Some negative people you can't avoid, such as family members. Most people have at least one family member with a propensity for negativity no matter what happens. You know the type. Even if they were to win a million dollars, they would complain about the income tax. They'll always be part of your family, but you can stop being bathed in their negativity. You can just stop listening to it. To this day, if someone texts or talks to me about a problem, if they're being overly negative, I might not even respond.

Some of my friends and family now catch themselves around me and realize what they're doing. They'll say, "Oops, I'm being negative. Sorry. Let me rephrase and be more positive." Once they make that change, I will fully engage with them and help fix the issue.

If you visit the in-laws and they start dumping negativity on you, it's time to go home or go take a walk. If someone in your family is telling you you're crazy for trying to become successful or you're stupid or you're doomed to fail, excuse yourself and leave. If they want to keep you down, just leave. You don't have to accept it, even from family.

You can't change other people. All you can do is tell them what you're doing, tell them how you feel, and if they don't accept it, leave. In the Bible, there's a passage that says if you preach the Word to someone and they don't receive it, knock the dust off your boots and go knock on the next door and tell the next person the good news. The point is that you cannot force people to behave a certain way, but you can move on.

When you have a spouse who creates the negative environment, it's a little trickier. You can't just be rid of everyone in your life who is important to you, but you can control the situation to some degree. You do that by being strong. I don't know why, but I see so many men these days who are more afraid of their wives saying no than of anything else. A lot of women are not strong enough either. You have to make some effort to control your environment the best you can.

What does that mean in practice? I have a sister whom I dearly love. She practically raised me, but in the past, she could be a negative force. Did I stop her from coming over to my house? No, because I love her, but I have made it clear to her that the conversation is over once she goes negative. I'll just look at her, smile, and walk away. She knows that, so she doesn't do it anymore. You don't have to participate. Today, though, she gets it and implements many of these same success principles. And it has paid off for her. By the way, my sister is one of the best people on the planet, and again, I love her dearly. No offense, Deb!

If someone in your life tries to drag you into their negative space, refuse to engage it. Make them understand where you're going instead. Block out the negative and try to convey the message that you're not going to buy into it. Period. Your efforts will be worth it. Your success depends on it.

CHAPTER FIVE

—

GAME TIME

After I took that three-day real estate investing class, after the week of training, and after my one-on-one mentorship with Cris, I was fired up. I was inspired, and it was game time. I knew that real estate investing was the vehicle I had been looking for to go along with my new beast mindset. With the knowledge that I now had, and with my new mind game, it was time to go for it.

When I first started investing in real estate, my goal was just to get out of debt. But after I gained my new mindset and knowledge, I raised my limitations. My goal was now to build and leave a legacy. It was time to go to the next level. Time to raise my limitations. I was determined never to become trapped in an active income environment again.

ONE DOOR AT A TIME

Your first door is the toughest because it's not real to you yet, it's not something you've done. It's only a theory you learned in class. It's something you've heard that's going to happen. Then the agent calls and says, "Your offer's been accepted." That's when you have your "Oh shit" moment. Now it's real.

After you do your first deal, you'll find that the second deal comes much easier. I don't fully know the explanation for that. I don't know if it's law of attraction or more confidence or if it's just the way the world works. Generally, your first door is the hardest, the most challenging, and the most exciting. You'll never forget it. Then they just keep coming, and you keep knocking them down. That's when you create momentum and build up your pipeline. I added one door at a time, and my business began to gain momentum and grow.

As I said before, my technology business was completely predicated on active income. The harder I worked, the more I sold, the more money I made. Just like with a normal job, if you put in overtime, you make more money. If you work less, you earn less. That's active income.

Passive income is an annuity. It's something that continues to pay you without your having to be there. I focused on single-family homes that I could buy and then rent out.

My net income was the rent minus the expenses. Plus, I bought in areas where the rental market was strong and produced the best passive income.

If you have a strong cash flow property, once you pay off the debt, it's mailbox money month after month forever. Even when the real estate market was bad and some people in the business worried that it would become even worse, I always said, "If the economy and the housing market sink further, what do people do? They rent." They don't buy properties, they don't buy homes for their families because they can't afford them, so they become renters. People have to live somewhere. If you have more renters in the market, you have a stronger asset.

When the economy recovers and the housing market goes back up, your property value increases too. In that situation, on top of collecting rent, you have the equity and appreciation of the real estate, so you've double-dipped. I made single-family residences my specialty because I wanted to build a business that I wouldn't lose even if the economy changed, even if the housing market went up, down, or sideways. No matter what, it would provide me with enough passive income for my basic needs.

THE 1 PERCENT RULE

When you're building a cash flow system, you have to

study the real estate market in the region you're targeting. You have to study the housing availability and home prices, consider the rental rates, look at the city's government and laws, and assess the local economy. Once you decide on a market to go into, you have to go there to build relationships with contractors and management companies.

When you're investing in cash flow, there is something called the 1 percent rule. The 1 percent rule is a basic starting point to help investors evaluate whether a property will work as a cash flow property. In general, if a property will not rent out for at least 1 percent of the purchase price, it is not a good cash flow property.

For example, a $100,000 home will have to bring in at least $1,000 per month in rent to be a good cash flow property. If market rents for that $100,000 property are only $750 per month, it may not work as a cash flow property. But if you can rent that $100,000 home for $1,200 per month, that is a solid cash flow property. The same goes for more expensive homes. A $500,000 home would have to bring in at least $5,000 per month to be considered a cash flow property. The 1 percent rule is a beginner guideline to know if you should even consider that property for a cash flow hold property. There is much more that goes into evaluating a solid cash flow property. That is why having the knowledge and educating yourself in this area is crucial.

As a real estate investor, you can and should invest in any part of the country where the numbers make sense. I live in Southern California, but I did not try to build my cash flow system there. The home prices are just too high, so the numbers usually don't make sense, especially when you're just starting out. For example, an $850,000 home in Los Angeles generally will not bring in 1 percent, or $8,500 per month, in rent. So the numbers don't work. Areas where the homes are very expensive often do not work as cash flow markets.

On the other end of the spectrum, low-income neighborhoods are also generally not good cash flow markets but for different reasons. In those areas, a property that you can purchase for $50,000 will often pass the 1 percent rule test, yielding $500 or more in monthly rent. But these markets tend to have a different set of problems.

First, properties in low-income areas rarely appreciate, so you don't get to double-dip by both collecting rent and having the home appreciate in value while you hold it. That takes away one of the biggest benefits of investing in real estate. Another significant problem in low-income markets is that the tenants often beat the hell out of the properties, so landlords tend to have very high annual maintenance and repair costs, which eliminates profit.

Generally, cash flow properties in low-income markets

have numbers that don't work. Owners find themselves continually pouring time and money into a bad situation. Nevertheless, the low price of homes in such areas is often tempting to inexperienced investors, and they make the mistake of buying inexpensive, cheap properties that they think will produce cash flow.

Wise cash flow investors focus on mid-priced areas. These are the cash flow markets that provide a good cash flow cap rate and have long-term renters who care for the property. They also tend to have solid appreciation, so investors can double-dip.

Of course, there is much more to learn about evaluating cash flow properties. I urge everyone to get proper training. Again, the 1 percent rule is the beginning baseline.

MY CHEESE MOVED

As I began gaining traction and buying more properties, I still co-owned my failing computer business with my partner. The business was in such bad shape financially I wasn't even taking an income from it for eighteen months. The computer company was continuing to tank, and it simply could not support two owners—it could barely support one owner. I approached my cousin and told him I wanted to move on and pursue real estate investing as a career. I signed an agreement letting my cousin have the computer business, and I basically walked away. I was now free to go all-in and pursue real estate full time.

However, I do not recommend that anyone walk away from a job and an income to invest in real estate. Please understand I had no choice: my cheese moved. Most people should keep their job and wait until they have a pipeline and income established.

> ## I DO NOT RECOMMEND THAT ANYONE WALK AWAY FROM A JOB AND AN INCOME TO INVEST IN REAL ESTATE.

Quitting a paying job to invest in real estate is almost always a bad idea because it leads to making bad decisions. Instead, build up your real estate knowledge, get proper training, gain experience, do some deals, get some money flowing in, and then you can consider whether or not to quit your day job. But establish some success and income in real estate first.

GOODBYE, 25,000-SQUARE-FOOT OFFICE. HELLO, STARBUCKS

When I left my computer business, I was deeply in debt, I had bad credit, and I didn't have money for an office. So the Starbucks coffee shop in Irvine, California, became my office. I would work out of Starbucks with my laptop computer and my phone. I would fly back and forth to cash flow markets to build the market and build out the infrastructure. Once I had it set up and running, I'd stay in California and let the system work.

This is what I call "building out your infrastructure" or "building your power team." The power team is the group of professionals that you depend on to handle each piece of your business no matter how many miles away you are from the property. Your power team includes your property management company, real estate agents, title companies, contractors, inspectors, appraisers, brokers, wholesalers, attorneys, and more.

Once you find these professionals, you vet them, check references, ask for referrals, and build relationships with them. You can do this over the phone, but I prefer to fly out and meet these people face-to-face and build my power team in person. But either works. Once those relationships are established, you can manage the whole cash flow operation remotely—in my case, from a Starbucks.

At this point, I wasn't providing properties for other people or for investors. I was buying for my own personal cash flow system.

All my friends thought I was nuts.

When they heard that I left my multimillion-dollar computer business to buy houses, they thought I had lost my mind. They knew I owned my own technology business in a 25,000-square-foot office with my logo on the side of the building, and now they saw me sitting alone in Starbucks with my laptop and a pad of paper. They had no idea about the emotional pain and carnage that I experienced in that building.

They didn't understand what I was trying to do, so they criticized me. I had a lot of naysayers and a lot of pushback and negativity when I started. But I used pattern interruption to banish those negative thoughts. I disregarded the people who were laughing at me behind my back. I pushed through it because I believed in what I was doing, and I was determined to succeed.

BUILDING MY CASH FLOW SYSTEM

I find that a lot of people don't really understand the cash flow engine I built and how I was able to buy these properties while I was in such a bad financial situation. Let me explain exactly how it worked.

When I originally started out with this strategy, I didn't have a lot of capital to work with. But I had a little remaining money on my home equity line. That's what I used to buy my first property.

I had identified Indianapolis as a solid cash flow market where there were lots of bargain properties. I could buy a house there that was in foreclosure for, let's say, $30,000. Houses were very inexpensive at that time. Plus, a lot of them were pretty beat-up. I would put maybe $10,000 or $15,000 into renovations to bring the property back up and make it a very nice-looking rental property. After the purchase price plus rehab expense, I would have a $50,000 all-in cost on a property. But at the time, due to the mechanics of that market, our appraisals were coming in really high. After these properties would get rehabbed, they would have an appraisal of sometimes up to $100,000. In theory, I would have $50,000 in equity.

The appraisals were really bullish at the time. That's part of what was fueling the real estate bubble from 2005 to 2008. The bubble was accelerated by very lenient lending and appraising standards. So I would take that $50,000 house, I would go get an appraisal on it for, let's say, $95,000 or $100,000, and I would immediately be able to call a bank, refinance the home, and take out $45,000 or $50,000 cash. We call this a cash-out refi.

Banks would loan up to 90 percent of the appraised value of the property, sometimes even 95 percent. When I did the cash-out refi, there was no seasoning. That means I didn't have to hold the property for any set amount of time before doing the cash-out refi. The lending guidelines were completely lax, even nonexistent.

Typically, I would get a loan on a property up to 95 percent of its value, which is called loan to value (LTV). That means for a house appraised at $100,000, I was getting a loan on the property for $95,000. I had $50,000 total invested in the property, and the bank would send me a check for up to $95,000. In other words, I would get my $50,000 back, plus an extra $45,000. Cash. They were letting owners strip all the equity because properties were going up so much, and that's what the guidelines were at the time.

I would have a property that was completely leveraged with a mortgage on it for $95,000. But I'd have an extra $50,000 in my pocket. What do you think I did with that extra $50,000? I bought another property. I paid cash for it. No mortgage, no debt.

That means I would have one house that was completely leveraged and one house that was paid for in cash with no mortgage. We would get anywhere from $750 to $1,050 in rent in these areas. If I got $1,000 in rent, that would cover my mortgage, insurance, taxes, and everything else. I was basically breaking even on the one that I leveraged; I wasn't making any positive cash flow on it. On the other property, I had no mortgage and no payment, but I still had that rent coming in.

I was clearing $700 a month after insurance, taxes, and paying the management company. That means I was cash-positive of $700 a month in passive mailbox money. I broke even on the one that I leveraged, but I was making $700 a month on the other one; meanwhile, both properties were appreciating and building value.

There were no guidelines on how many of these a borrower could do. So I started just duplicating that system over and over. Once again, I saw the power of duplication. I'd buy one that was leveraged and break even on it, and have one that was profiting $700 a month. I got up to about twenty of these properties; ten of them were producing $700 a month. It was $7,000 a month cash flow. Not bad.

CHEESE MOVED, AGAIN

Now remember, I was still buried in millions of dollars of debt, so I wasn't solving my bigger problem. But at least I had income. It was a one-door-at-a-time concept that was slowly getting me to where I was trying to go. My goal was to own a lot of real estate, build a lot of assets, create passive income, and slowly work my way out of debt. It worked well, and I was pretty excited about the cash flow machine I was building.

Then, like everything else, something changes, and your cheese gets moved. Here's what happened. The banks started to get a lot of these properties back in foreclosure because some unscrupulous borrowers were doing what I was doing, a cash-out refi, but they were just pocketing the cash and walking away from the properties and letting them go to foreclosure. They were basically stealing the equity out of the properties. Of course, I wasn't doing that; I had ethics, and I had a goal of building a lot of assets.

The banks got hurt pretty bad by this, so they put a stop to it. Mortgage lenders went into lockdown mode. The cash-out refi loans dried up. It became almost impossible to borrow money to buy real estate. Once again, my cheese moved.

I knew I could still operate my cash flow system, but I needed a new strategy. Getting bank loans was no longer an option. How was I going to buy properties to hold and create mailbox money without borrowing from banks? That was my goal—I wanted to be a cash flow guy. I wanted to hold single-family rentals. But I needed a new source of capital.

THE NAYSAYERS WANTED SOME CHEESE

The same folks who were those naysayers saw the passive income I was making, and they began to take an interest in what I was doing. When I showed them the returns I was getting on my investments, they were intrigued.

I explained to them how I was buying properties and holding the inventory and collecting rent. When they realized the potential, some of those same naysayers began asking, "Could you do one of these for me? Could you buy one for us?"

It took me a while, but that's when the light bulb went off. I thought, "Wow! I can do these for other people. Maybe I should start thinking bigger than just doing this for myself. Maybe if I do this for somebody else, I can expand faster." That's when it hit me that I had something others needed and wanted. See, my training, knowledge, contacts, and inventory had a massive value, and it was time to cash in on that. And best of all, it was a huge win for the investor. Win-win!

The first time I flipped one of these properties to an investor, I had my "Oh shit" moment. I made thousands of dollars for only ten or twenty hours of work. Nice! So I did two more, and I received a referral. Then I did five, ten, fifteen more. I was making on average of $10,000 per flip.

With investors' money, I started to buy in greater quantity than a typical individual investor would be able to because I'd already built the system. I was starting to pick up momentum. I was saving my investors' money because I knew where to buy, what to buy, and how to buy. I also knew how to get better pricing on construction and renovation, and better pricing on management. I had the machine already built, so anyone who bought from me would benefit from that. If they had to re-create that infrastructure on their own, it would take months and cost a lot of money; it would lower or even eliminate their profit.

I knew my system offered considerable value to investors right out of the gate. Let me explain the numbers from the investor's standpoint. If I had invested a total of $70,000 in a property to buy it, rehab it, and put a renter in it, I'd be able to sell it to an investor for $80,000, so I'd make $10,000 on the sale. It was good for the buyer because if they went out on their own, they wouldn't know what property to buy, they wouldn't know what area to buy in, and they wouldn't know how to do the rehab. Nor would they know where to find the management. In fact, they probably wouldn't even buy something that was two thousand miles away from where they lived because they wouldn't have the infrastructure or the comfort level. If they tried to do this on their own, they'd probably spend $90,000 or more. I was well worth the $10,000.

I cranked up the machine, and the operation began to grow. I just kept buying as much inventory as I could and kept the engine going by selling them to investors. Once again, it was the power of duplication and the strength in numbers—more investors means more buying power. I kept duplicating the system over and over.

Here's the power in creating this system. Each investor got a solid investment with a nice 8 to 12 percent return on their money, and I made $10,000 per property. After selling ten properties to investors, I would have $100,000 in liquid cash. After twenty properties, I'd have $200,000. I took that cash and invested it in four new properties for myself. Those four properties would generate about $2,800 per month in passive income. While I was turning a profit for my investors, I was also building up my own personal cash flow portfolio. I just kept turning the wheel and cranking the machine. I was also able to now start supporting myself again and start paying off my massive debts.

AFTER TWENTY PROPERTIES, I'D HAVE $200,000. I TOOK THAT CASH AND INVESTED IT IN FOUR NEW PROPERTIES FOR MYSELF.

A TURNKEY SYSTEM

I made investing in real estate easy for people who had no experience in it. I was providing buyers with a full-service turnkey system—basically a wholesale flip, if you will. I even provided what type of insurance to put on each property with which insurance company. You have to have those relationships with vendors and contractors and management companies built, and that takes time and effort. But once it's built, any investor you work with can benefit from it. The investors only had to write a check; I did the rest.

This turnkey system was ideal for any investor who wanted to put their money to work in a piece of real estate that was a cash flow rental. The investor could buy real estate with the full support of myself, my team on the ground, and all of our knowledge, relationships, and protection. With little effort or work, they could buy a fully functioning asset that would provide them a nice cap rate and that could appreciate over time. It was basically investing money in real estate safely through a tried-and-true system.

I began expanding the cash flow business in that direction. I did another one and another one and then another one. Those investors referred more people, and then I did a few more. I started picking up momentum because people wanted to invest their money in real estate; they just didn't know how. They didn't have the knowledge or the infrastructure, so they would either fall back on investing in mutual funds or do nothing.

Turnkey real estate investing filled a niche in the market.

HOOSIER CASH FLOW MARKET

The main cash flow market I focused on in the beginning was Indiana. The state was run very well, and Indianapolis in particular was an attractive cash flow market. Mitch Daniels was the governor at the time, and he was doing a great job. The government was in the black financially.

Indiana was very business friendly and investor friendly, had low taxes, and low city violations. It was a great place for real estate investors. Because Indianapolis was a linear market, properties would hold their value. The rents were strong. There were a lot of jobs. Eli Lilly, the pharmaceutical company, was there, and a lot of big companies were moving there. There was a lot of opportunity. The economy there was strong, and the middle-class properties made great cash flow holds.

It took some time, but I forged a relationship with a savvy local investor there who knew how to buy properties at auction and understood the market, and whom I could create a partnership with to build my cash flow machine.

I HAVE A FACE FOR RADIO

I sat in that Starbucks with a laptop and ran my cash flow system. And drank too many lattes. I was making good money, but I was still deep in debt, and I was working out of a coffee shop. I knew there was more. I knew I had to expand. I just needed to get the word out somehow. From 2004 to 2008, the real estate industry was scorching hot. Timing was on my side but not for long.

If you remember that time, you might recall that everyone was getting into the mortgage business because mortgage brokers were making a killing. They were becoming millionaires and driving Ferraris. Everyone chased the greed. But just like any other bubble boom, it eventually went bust.

In 2008, the mortgage industry and the subprime loan market imploded, and the big real estate bubble began to burst. The banks went from giving loans to anybody with a pulse to practically requiring an act of Congress to get a loan because of all the new regulations.

Most of the mortgage brokers went out of business. But there were these four mortgage brokers who had a radio show called *The Round Table* on 97.1 FM in Los Angeles. On weekends, they talked about the mortgage industry and promoted their business. When their mortgage business went belly-up, they wanted to keep the show, but they could no longer promote mortgages. They didn't know what to do, so they started contacting real estate investors to have them promote their deals on air. They took a cut of the profits from each deal. They used radio as their marketing tool.

A mutual acquaintance who knew me and knew the radio show guys contacted me and asked me to meet with them. We met, and I told them what I was doing. We agreed to terms, and they invited me on the radio. I came onto their show as a guest. They gave me a limited amount of time to talk about what I was doing. Then they asked me a few questions and gave out my number. That first guest spot led to others, and I started moving inventory through their show and paying them a commission on the sales.

I figured, "Hey, they're paying for the marketing, I'm moving properties, and investors are getting solid investment opportunities." It was a win for the *Round Table* guys. It was a win for me. It was a win for the investors who got the properties because they're good properties. It was a good relationship.

I started selling more properties than ever. Every time I would pick up an investor, that would lead to another couple of investors through word of mouth because what I did actually worked. It was a great return. People wanted to do real estate investing, but they didn't know how. I helped them do it. I started doing many properties a month, and I was creating a lot of revenue and momentum.

As always, I was investing the profits back into my personal cash flow properties. I wasn't blowing it on depreciating assets because I learned about money intelligence. My whole goal was to build up mailbox money and find a passive revenue source. To be able to keep doing that, you have to have a system. I just kept working my system and building my wealth one door at a time.

I JUST KEPT WORKING MY SYSTEM AND BUILDING MY WEALTH ONE DOOR AT A TIME.

GREED DEALS

The four guys who ran *The Round Table* radio show started promoting some real estate deals on their show with other investors whom I thought were highly suspect. For example, one was in Ocala, Florida, and it was a preconstruction deal. At that point, preconstruction was dead, so people were getting screwed big-time by those deals. Preconstruction is new builds. The market was now being flooded with old inventory, so the last thing you'd want to do is build more inventory at that time. Simple supply and demand. I warned the guys, "Hey, with this deal in Ocala, you're going to have major egg on your face. I looked it over. Whoever gets into these kinds of deals is going to get screwed. It will destroy your reputation and hurt the investors." I call any real estate deal that one knows is bad but will give to someone else a "greed deal."

I CALL ANY REAL ESTATE DEAL THAT ONE KNOWS IS BAD BUT WILL GIVE TO SOMEONE ELSE A "GREED DEAL."

They didn't listen because they were hurting and needed money. They continued promoting those kinds of suspect deals, so I made an integrity decision. I pulled myself off their show. I didn't want to be associated with it because I knew something bad was going to happen. It was a decision I made on principle even though it hurt me financially.

I basically broke the relationship with those guys. But I knew that reputation and integrity is everything. People listening to their radio show didn't know who was who on the show. I worried that I was going to be associated with these other shady deals somehow, even though I had nothing to do with them. I warned them, and I got myself away from it. Ultimately, that project in Ocala, Florida, went belly-up. Their reputation took a hit, and they had a big mess on their hands. Luckily, I got out of there before it all went down.

Then I thought, "Hey, if these four knuckleheads can do a radio show, why can't I?" If I had my own radio show, I could control the whole hour. Yeah, I'll have the costs and the overhead. Yes, I will have to pay. It's very expensive to get on radio and do paid programming, but hey, if I sell enough properties and it's just focused on me and my system, maybe I can sell even more properties. Then the cost won't be a factor. To achieve success, you have to be willing to invest in yourself and your business.

TO ACHIEVE SUCCESS, YOU HAVE TO BE WILLING TO INVEST IN YOURSELF AND YOUR BUSINESS.

THE NV RADIO SHOW

I took a calculated risk. I started investigating how to get on the air. I hired a rep, and she helped me land my own show.

When I first got the show, they tried to tell me how to run it. They told me to talk a certain way and say certain things. They wanted to make me into a radio personality. They said I needed guests. I had all these radio folks tell me, "You have to talk like this. You have to say this. You have to run your show like this if you want listenership." But it just didn't feel right to me. I've always been a guy who likes to just shoot straight and do things my own way. I always listen to my instincts.

I ALWAYS LISTEN TO MY INSTINCTS.

I thought to myself, "Bullshit. People want to hear the truth from someone who is authentic and real. I'm just going to tell them what I do. I'm going to promote my turnkey business. But I'm also going to give them genuine real estate knowledge. I'm going to tell them what's happening out there, because nobody's telling them the truth." I wanted to do radio my way.

PEOPLE WANT TO HEAR THE TRUTH FROM SOMEONE WHO IS AUTHENTIC AND REAL.

So that's exactly what I did. I had one hour on the air on Saturdays, and the program aired on multiple stations. I decided to talk about what I would want to hear, what I would want to listen to, if I were tuning in to a real estate show. I went against the grain of the "experts," and I started doing things my way on the show.

At first, I had a lot of people call in saying I was crazy, but then everything I had predicted began to happen. The key to my success was that I truly understood the market. I understood what was really happening on the ground. I was authentic, and I kept it real by telling people the truth. My listenership started to grow. I began doing very well. My phones started ringing off the hook for my product.

I became the number one real estate radio show in Southern California for paid programming. Suddenly, everyone wanted to advertise on my show, which made my costs go way down. I was doing great. The show was called *The Real Estate Investing Hour*. I gave my listeners real-world advice, and I offered them opportunities to invest. It was a powerful business arrangement in which everyone involved benefited.

THE BEST KEPT SECRETS: IRAS AND 401(K)S

When I was doing the radio show, about 85 percent of my investors bought properties through their individual retirement accounts. Yes, their IRAs. That's where most people in the United States have the majority of their money. The typical IRA is invested in low-yield mutual funds or risky stocks. The concept of investing a retirement account in tangible, real property is attractive to many investors.

Most people don't know before I educate them that you can invest in real estate within your IRA. You can flip and buy a rental property with that money. This is one of the best-kept secrets in retirement savings. It's surprising to me how few people know this. As I mentioned in chapter 2, financial institutions and investment advisers often don't educate their clients about this for a couple of reasons.

THIS IS ONE OF THE BEST-KEPT SECRETS IN RETIREMENT SAVINGS. IT'S SURPRISING TO ME HOW FEW PEOPLE KNOW THIS.

First, financial advisers might have the best of intentions, but most of them just don't understand real estate investing. They're much more knowledgeable about stocks, bonds, CDs, money market accounts, and mutual funds, so that's what they tend to recommend to their clients. Second, some financial advisers are looking out for their own best interests. They want to earn commissions by selling mutual funds and stocks to their clients. Real estate does not generate any commissions for them. So they fail to mention it.

Let me give you a simple explanation of how investing retirement money in a cash flow hold property works. Let's say, for easy math, the property costs $100,000 and you have $100,000 in your IRA. The money gets wired out of your IRA, and then it goes to escrow. You now own the property outright because you paid cash and there is no mortgage, and it's inside of your IRA because you're allowed to own properties in an IRA. Most people don't know that. It's the best-kept secret out there. Financial institutions and financial planners don't want you to know this because they don't want to lose their commissions on stocks and mutual funds.

You can hold gold, you can hold art, you can hold a lot of things in an IRA, but real estate is one of the smartest assets you can acquire. I teach this to all of my investors in my classes. Instead of going to the last page of your quarterly IRA statement to make sure your $100,000 is there, instead of seeing all those mutual funds that you don't know what the hell they are, you see a physical property address. The rental income is coming right back into your IRA.

All the profit that goes back into the IRA is tax deferred, so you don't pay taxes on it until you use the money. If your property value goes from $100,000 to $150,000, your IRA is now is worth $150,000, plus the rental income that you have acquired while you held the property. You control the real estate, so you could sell the property at any time. When you sell it, the $150,000 gets wired right back into your retirement account, plus all the money you made from your rent, minus expenses.

You can make 8 to 12 percent on your money, and it's a brick-and-mortar asset that won't disappear in a stock market crash. A brick-and-mortar physical asset is a smart way to hold your money. Most American families have two breadwinners, with both parents working full time. It's not like the old days. You can't just work your way to retirement. Either you have to be a high earner, or you have to invest your way there. All you need is the knowledge, the training, the support, and the network to invest wisely.

MOST AMERICAN FAMILIES HAVE TWO BREADWINNERS, WITH BOTH PARENTS WORKING FULL TIME. IT'S NOT LIKE THE OLD DAYS. YOU CAN'T JUST WORK YOUR WAY TO RETIREMENT.

What if the real estate in your IRA gets destroyed or damaged? Good question. I once had an investor whose property burned down. Fortunately, he had the right insurance because we made sure through our system that he did. His property was rebuilt, and he was paid rent during the time it was being rebuilt.

The project came in $10,000 under budget, and he put the extra money back in his pocket. He had $10,000 cash in his pocket and a brand-new house, and he never missed the rent. What's the downside? It can't disappear; it's a house. It's brick and mortar. People are always going to rent, even when things are bad.

E-TICKET: RIDE THE MOMENTUM

The radio show grew to become a great moneymaker for me. All of a sudden, I was moving a ton of properties, fifteen or twenty a month, just from the radio show. Also, I was selling many more through word-of-mouth referrals because my cash flow system worked. I had no radio or communications training, but I would just speak from the heart on air. I didn't write anything out. I just took ten bullet points at a time and talked about what I was seeing in the market, my properties, and my system.

For years, I sold properties that way through my system and on the radio. Every time I'd make profits from the show, I'd buy more personal rental properties in order to keep building my passive income portfolio. I never wanted to be in the horrible place I was after I lost my computer business, so my motivation was fear, but it was a healthy, controlled fear.

I knew what not to do. I knew not to create massive overhead with an active income business because the second the music stops, you're in trouble. That's what I had done in the past, but I'd learned my lesson. From now on, I would do things the smart way.

Not many people were doing it like I was doing it. I was one of the top guys out there operating at this level. It was amazing to me that just a few years earlier, I knew nothing about real estate. I was down on my luck, so I went through a three-day real estate event. I had no money and was millions in debt. My credit sucked because of all the debt, and I was behind on my bills and financially buried. It was about the worst situation I could imagine.

I focused on grinding every day. I used pattern interruption to replace the negative chatter in the back of my mind. I was determined to succeed. My hard work began to pay off.

One thing I've learned is that as you start to pick up momentum, you have to ride the wave as long as you can. You have to put your foot on the gas, keep going, and keep grinding. When my business picked up, I didn't lose focus or start focusing on other things or other projects. I found this particular niche, and I wanted to just hammer it because it was working. I stayed focused, and I rode the wave.

ONE THING I'VE LEARNED IS THAT AS YOU START TO PICK UP MOMENTUM, YOU HAVE TO RIDE THE WAVE AS LONG AS YOU CAN. YOU HAVE TO PUT YOUR FOOT ON THE GAS, KEEP GOING, AND KEEP GRINDING.

I was still millions of dollars in debt, but at least I had a profit-making vehicle and I was slowly working my way out of it. I took my medicine for all the mistakes I made. I could finally see light at the end of the tunnel.

I was not an overnight success in real estate. I was in it for the long haul, and it was a long hustle. I put my head down, focused, and kept the machine running and kept moving forward. The pain of my past mistakes was finally beginning to fade in the rearview mirror.

Unfortunately, the worst struggle of my life was yet to come.

WARNING: THIS GETS PERSONAL

I need to pause here and give the reader a warning. In this section of the book, I'm going to reveal the raw, embarrassing truth about a very dark chapter in my life. I'm going to bare my soul. I'm going to tell you the unfiltered details of my personal story because I want you to understand where the lessons and ideas in this book come from. This book isn't full of stuff that I researched in a library or learned from interviewing other entrepreneurs. It happened to me.

And it devastated me.

But I bounced back, and I'm now stronger and more successful than ever. I want readers to understand that you can and will survive demoralizing setbacks and crushing defeats, and you can use them to grow and feed your future success. I'm going to share details with you that I don't share with many people. I'm going to expose myself, my fears, my emotions, and what I went through when this happened to me.

As you have gathered by now, I am a strong-minded person who focuses on the positive, not the negative. Even though the tale you're about to read is not the most positive, it must be understood so you can fully grasp the lessons coming later in the book. The lessons about business and life that I explain in this book grew out of my experiences, including the darkest chapter of my life. If you thought the collapse of my technology business was rough, wait until you read the next chapter. Again, this isn't to focus on the negative; this is to share a difficult chapter of my life so you can know what it took for me to get to the top, where I am today. It's for you, the reader, to see how sometimes success can be had no matter what you're up against or who is trying to stop you.

The people you're about to read about are not a factor in my life anymore; I have moved on with gratitude for the lessons learned and because their negative actions actually fueled my success. This is a story about persevering and overcoming. My hope is that it will inspire you to overcome whatever obstacles you're facing in your life.

I'm not going to be using real names, partly because the

people involved don't even deserve their names to be mentioned. At one time, we were the closest of friends, which is why writing this and reliving it brings back so many emotions. I'm going to use made-up names. One of the key people in the story loved tacos, so I'm going to call him Taco Montenegro. The other key person in this story I'll call Geno Fernando.

These two former best friends of mine tried to destroy me. Well, one did, and one betrayed me out of fear for himself. But in so doing, they empowered me. They put me in the place where I am today. What they put me through was the worst thing that ever happened to me, yet because of what I learned and how I responded, it wound up being the best thing to ever happen to me.

Why was it the best thing? Because it helped me understand what I'm capable of, what I can handle, and how broad my shoulders really are to handle anything that life throws at me. It made me even more who I am today, all because of this challenge, because of this negative experience in my life. As I tell you the gut-wrenching story, I'm doing it so you understand that I'm not just giving you theoretical success concepts in this book. I lived through it and overcame it, and that's what makes this book special. That's what makes this different from most people who write these types of books.

I want you to get to the core of what I felt and what I was

feeling when it was happening. To do that, I have to tell a story with a lot of personal detail. So let me tell you that story.

Trust me, these two people are in my rearview mirror today. I don't dwell on what happened, and I have no bitterness about it. It made me who I am, it built my business, and it drove me to the top of my industry. I owe them both a debt of gratitude.

I'm not writing this book because I'm still dwelling on the past. It's not me whining about what happened. I am writing this book because I want you to know how I got here, and what it takes to get here. This story just happens to be a crucial part of my journey.

So you're going to get the story raw. If there are a few words that offend you in this section, please know that I'm giving you this story unfiltered and real. I run a professional, classy business in every way; seldom will you hear a swear word at one of my events. But to fully understand this story, you have to hear it exactly how it happened.

Sharing this story is my way of showing you that no matter what comes your way, you can overcome it. Your destiny is what you make it, and if you want to be successful, you're going to have challenges. They may be smaller than this. They may be bigger. I don't know who you are, but I do know this is how life works, and I don't want to gloss over a section that's filled with life lessons just because it's an uncomfortable story to tell.

So strap in for one hell of a ride, take a breath, and turn the page.

CHAPTER SIX

—

MY DEAL WITH EL DIABLO

In 2009, I got a phone call that would change my life.

Back at that first three-day real estate seminar I took a few years earlier, I met one of the instructors named Chris Sanderson and struck up a friendship with him. This was a different guy than Cris, who did the one-on-one mentoring with me. One day, Chris Sanderson called me up. He had heard about what I was doing with my cash flow system, and he was impressed.

Chris said, "I'm working for another real estate training company. I just started a few months ago, and the guy who runs it has a TV show about flipping houses." Chris told me his name. "Have you heard of him?"

"No, I haven't," I said. "I don't watch those shows."

"Well," Chris said, "he's teaching people how to flip properties. The one thing I know he doesn't have is a cash flow curriculum to teach students how to create passive income. He only teaches people how to flip. I told him about you and your system, and how great it would be if you could teach cash flow to his students. I don't know, maybe there's something there. Maybe you guys could work together. He needs a guy with your expertise. Would you be willing to meet him?"

It sounded interesting, so I agreed to meet Taco Montenegro. We met, we liked each other, and over a four-and-a-half-year period, we built a relationship and trust. We decided to combine forces and work together.

CASH FLOW ON STEROIDS

Montenegro and I each owned our own businesses at the time, and we each brought value to our new joint venture. Montenegro was able to leverage his TV show and bring in students to his trainings. I brought two important things he didn't have: a cash flow curriculum and the ability to provide turnkey cash flow properties to his students.

In our new venture, Montenegro continued to teach students how to flip, and I taught a three-day cash flow course. For students who didn't have the time or interest in setting up their own cash flow system, I could provide them with properties. The students could buy properties from me and plug into my system, which included getting the property fully rehabbed, placing a renter in it, property management, and ongoing support.

From 2009 to 2013, we sold hundreds, if not thousands, of properties to Montenegro's students. Usually, the students would come through my three-day course, so they would learn the system and know what they were doing. Most of these students not only got the education, but they also had access to buy my turnkey cash flow properties, which in turn was generating millions of dollars in revenue for Montenegro's company.

In addition to selling properties through my joint venture with Montenegro, I was still doing my radio show. I was selling properties on my own through that channel as well. At my peak, between both channels, I was selling between thirty to seventy properties per month!

There was just one problem. In all the excitement, I failed to do one important thing. Somehow, I never signed any legal agreements, never received any shares, and never put anything in writing to protect myself and my sweat equity within this arrangement. We did the whole joint venture deal on a handshake. That was a temporary mistake. But ultimately, it turned out to be a blessing. I'll explain why.

Nevertheless, our system ran flawlessly. Four and a half years later, Montenegro and I had become such close friends that I was the executor of his estate. We were as tight as two friends could be. (Well, I thought we were.) That's what makes this such a hard story to tell.

You have to really understand the depths of our friendship for this to really make you feel the sting later. I honestly don't know how to write the words to make you feel it as deeply as I did. I had his back big-time, and I cared about our friendship massively. If I'm being really honest, I think I was one of his only true friends. He didn't make friends too easily, and he was impossible to deal with at times. Nevertheless, he grew on me, and I valued our friendship.

WHAT HAPPENS IN VEGAS STAYS IN VEGAS

When I first began working with Montenegro, I was providing properties in Indianapolis, where I had another on-the-ground partner. Indianapolis is a linear market, which means it doesn't go high or low; it just maintains. It's a great cash flow market. I was able to buy properties there at the right prices, rehab them at low cost, and earn solid rent. The economy was strong there, and we had a lot of success. Altogether, we did hundreds of properties in that market.

In contrast to a linear market like Indianapolis, right

before the bubble burst in 2008, Las Vegas and Orlando were hypermarkets. That means the real estate prices there were skyrocketing. Orlando has Disney and tourism, and Vegas has the casinos, tourism, and Zappos. The weather in both places is nice, even with the heat, so during the boom, real estate prices went up, up, up. But after the bubble burst in 2008, single-family middle-class houses that had been selling for $300,000 were now selling at auction for $50,000.

That's how far and fast the market went down. Vegas had become an amazing cash flow market with potential for huge appreciation as well. All real estate is local, and you have to work in the markets where the numbers are right. You can't buy a property at $300,000 and then rent it out for $1,300. That's a negative cash flow. But if you buy a property for $50,000, put $20,000 into it, and then charge between $950 and $1,300 in rent, you've created a nice source of positive cash flow.

I saw the opportunity in Las Vegas, and I knew we needed to jump on it. There was this young, bushy-browed guy named Geno Fernando who was working within Montenegro's company who was currently investing in Las Vegas and already had some momentum there. Geno was a very talented investor and he knew Vegas, so he was the ideal person for me to partner with to build my infrastructure there. But he was working with Montenegro at the time.

I asked Montenegro if Geno and I could partner together to build my cash flow engine in Vegas. Montenegro agreed. Geno and I formed a partnership, and once again sealed it with only a verbal agreement and a handshake. Big mistake on my part. But again, it worked out for the better ultimately.

Together, Geno and I built up Vegas into a massive operation. Over two years, we did hundreds of properties together. We hit that real estate market so hard and bought so much, we basically left a carcass in Vegas. We bought and renovated more properties than anybody out there. I kept the Indianapolis operation going too. All of the properties in those two cities were managed ongoing, so I didn't have to be hands-on.

We renovated so many properties that the city of Las Vegas actually wanted to name a special day after us, if you can believe that. Even though Geno and I did all the investing and all the buying, Montenegro found out about it, and somehow, he took all the credit. The city proclaimed an official Taco Montenegro Day. He loved the attention, so we let him have it even though he had nothing to do with the investing portion of it. Geno and I always had a good laugh about that.

This drove Geno bananas. Geno and Montenegro hated each other, by the way. They were like the same person but a little different. Both had to be the smartest guy in the room. Montenegro had massive hidden insecurity issues. Maybe that's why they always boasted and bragged. I used to have to keep them separated from each other. My whole goal was to keep this engine running and not have personalities get in the way. I was able to do that for a couple of years, and we were killing it.

Around the end of 2012 or the beginning of 2013, the inventory in Vegas began drying up. At the same time, the numbers in Orlando started becoming stronger. So we decided to launch in Orlando.

Geno and I went and created the same cash flow system in Orlando. Prices in Orlando were in the $50,000 to $70,000 range, so we started rehabbing and renting them. We could charge $1,000 to $1,500 in rent and get it easily. That market was so hot that Geno and his wife actually moved to Orlando so he could be our on-the-ground guy there, just as he was in Vegas. Orlando was going to be our next Vegas.

It was an exciting time, and I loved every minute of it. I was making a lot of money with the cash flow system, and I was having an absolute blast up on stage teaching my system to students and in my two friendships with Montenegro and Geno. Little did I know it would all come crashing down on my head and leave me wondering what the hell happened. My cheese was about to be moved—again.

LITTLE DID I KNOW IT WOULD ALL COME CRASHING DOWN ON MY HEAD AND LEAVE ME WONDERING WHAT THE HELL HAPPENED. MY CHEESE WAS ABOUT TO ME MOVED—AGAIN.

THE FISH STINKS AT THE HEAD

When I started working with Montenegro, I did a lot of teaching, speaking, and raising money for the massive inventory we needed for the demand we had. My business partner Geno did the on-the-ground stuff, such as finding the properties, buying them with our capital, and managing them. He was also raising capital for our system. He was more behind the scenes, while I was the face of the cash flow business, although Geno did do a lot of the teaching too and often provided me with many of the market and property facts of our inventory.

Geno was a brilliant investor. The kid was sharp as a tack. He was a great asset and partner as far as someone on the ground buying these properties and managing them. He was brilliant, but he was a dick.

The problem with Geno is that he had no people skills at all. Zero. He was cocky, couldn't hold his tongue, had a temper, and did not know how to build a business relationship with people. Even with me, he could not control his arrogance or his temper. That would cause major problems later.

There's an old Italian saying that goes like this: The fish stinks at the head. Leadership trickles down from the top. Neither Montenegro nor Geno had a heart for the students. They were both too cocky and self-centered, so taking care of the students fell to me on the property side of things. It was all me and my staff. I put together the sales process and the after-service. I was responsible not only for protecting my name and brand but also Montenegro's name and brand for that portion of his business, again from the property sales side. He was on his own on the training side, and well, as you will hear later, he failed miserably there.

THERE'S AN OLD ITALIAN SAYING THAT GOES LIKE THIS: THE FISH STINKS AT THE HEAD. LEADERSHIP TRICKLES DOWN FROM THE TOP.

My strength is that I care for the students. I have an ability to communicate with them, and they put their trust in me. The reason students bought properties from us was because they believed in me and because when they had a problem, I stepped up and handled it. In contrast, Montenegro's people never even called anybody back in regard to the training his company was selling them. My ability to build relationships, communicate a message, and lead and run a company are my biggest assets. I play long ball and protect my name.

Geno's tendency was to tell clients to fuck off. I couldn't

allow that because my name was on it now, and Montenegro's name was on it. We fought daily about how to treat the clients. I demanded we treat them with respect and build long-lasting relationships. I protected the clients, and in so doing, I protected our interests too.

YOUNG AND COCKY

As mentioned, Geno did a lot of the teaching too, because he was a talented real estate investor and had most of the market knowledge. However, the students were drawn to me because they knew I had a heart for them. That's why we were successful, not because we knew numbers or because the properties were exceptional. We were successful because students believed that I had their best interests at heart and that I cared.

Over time, as our partnership evolved, what I taught Geno was, first of all, how to present himself on stage because he had to teach a lot of the sections. Plus, people had to get to know him because he was the person on the ground who was going to manage the property, so he had to be presentable and agreeable.

At first, Geno sucked on stage while presenting because of his horrible presence: he was too cocky and arrogant. The students could sense it. I had to figure out a way to fix it. I molded the guy basically into being a passable version of himself that would be at least acceptable. He grew to be better and better over time. I think when he saw the revenue we were generating, he would have taught on stage in a dress if he had to.

I even had to sit on stage with him during his presentations, and every time he'd say something condescending to the students, I would chime in: "He's just kidding." I tried to make a joke out of it, and usually the students would laugh. But Geno had horrible bedside manners. I had to coach him constantly.

When Geno didn't want to service a student or a customer because he felt he was right, I was the one who had to step in. I had a final say on what we did and what we didn't do with the students because I knew how to play long ball. I worry about my reputation. I worry about what's going to get out there on the street.

Geno realized he was getting valuable mentorship from me, and he was willing to go along with it because he saw the momentum we were picking up. We did hundreds of properties together.

MASSIVE CASH FLOW ENGINE

In Geno, I found a business partner who complemented my strengths and made up for my weaknesses. The guy understood real estate, he understood numbers. He did a lot of the things that bored me stiff. He was good at it, and we were a great partnership.

We did this for a couple of years, creating a massive cash flow engine by raising millions of dollars and rehabbing hundreds of properties and putting renters in them. We did 840 properties in two years between Orlando and Vegas. Geno was really great at what he did, better than what I could be because he was just wired that way. That was his strength; that was his lane.

Geno and I became very close. We both came to appreciate each other and what we both brought to the partnership. I believe, at least from my side, we became very close friends. I will tell you this: I was very loyal to Montenegro, but I also had Geno's back unconditionally.

As I alluded to earlier, unfortunately, there was a problem. Geno was hotheaded, and he had a huge ego. His personality flaws, especially his hidden fear, would lead to both of our undoing and eventually lead to the end of our friendship.

TROUBLE WAS BREWING

Montenegro was an egomaniac. Everything was about serving him, never serving the students or the great people who helped him build his company. He didn't treat customers with respect. He didn't care about them. I really don't think he ever even had a customer service department. Montenegro's idea of customer service is to never call anyone back and hope the customer goes away. Because Montenegro did not run his company professionally and didn't protect his brand, his bad press became horrendous. His reputation was bad when I met him, and it only got worse.

A good leader should never forget the people who bring value. But Montenegro didn't see things that way. The people who helped him build his company never received any credit and often were devalued. This is a huge mistake when building a company, and it hurt him more than he will ever know or admit.

Montenegro was stubborn and arrogant, and he thought no matter what was said about him in the press, he was the great Taco Montenegro and his business would be just fine. Well, business doesn't work that way. If you treat your customers and staff with disdain, you won't have them for very long. When dealing with customers, you need to come from a place of service. Staff need to feel respected and valued, and they should have a deep respect for their leader as well, not disdain and fear.

In 2012, Montenegro's business started to suffer from

all the mismanagement. He had a big losing year. He confided in me that he took a financial beating in 2012. He didn't even realize he was taking a beating until halfway through the year because he had low-paid minions working for him, and they were afraid to tell him the bad news. He found out way after he should have that he was bleeding out financially and that his company was losing money. He tightened up on things and tried to cut costs, but it was too little too late. Let me rephrase that: he went into panic greed mode and started executing good people within his company. He was chewing off his own limbs and creating bad blood and focusing on the wrong things. His approach was horrendous at best.

Then all hell broke loose with Montenegro in the middle of 2012 and into 2013. He told me, "Make sure you don't say anything, but the training side of the business is tanking."

However, Geno and I were still selling a lot of properties. We were one of the only profitable parts of the company. I think Montenegro hated the fact that Geno and I were still killing it, while he was failing.

Montenegro got really angry, ornery, and made a lot of deep cuts as he tried to right the ship. But I think his reputation was too far gone by that point. I don't think he realized that at the time. He focused on cutting costs and cutting people's pay, including what he and I originally agreed to.

It was the first time I saw how poorly Montenegro handled adversity and how selfish he was when making decisions that affect others. What bothered me is not that he had to make those tough decisions. Every business owner has to make difficult decisions that impact other people. But those decisions should always be made with honesty, integrity, and class.

Montenegro didn't operate that way.

EVERY BUSINESS OWNER HAS TO MAKE DIFFICULT DECISIONS THAT IMPACT OTHER PEOPLE. BUT THOSE DECISIONS SHOULD ALWAYS BE MADE WITH HONESTY, INTEGRITY, AND CLASS.

Montenegro could have come to me and said, "Here is the situation: we need to rework the agreement because my numbers aren't working anymore." Of course, nobody likes their agreements changed or being told they're going to make less money. But if he had explained it to me, I would have understood and agreed. Sadly, Montenegro didn't have the class or the balls to handle it that way. Instead, he showed up to a cash flow event in summer 2012 and fabricated a list of things he felt were wrong with the event. He went on an aggressive tirade at the event. He implied he would be taking over cash flow and no longer be paying anyone to teach it. He tried to sell the fact that he would drive more sales of properties so it would all work out. Bottom line: he said he wasn't paying me for the teaching anymore, and that's how he handled it. Again, I agree he had to cut that cost, but how he handled it was the beginning blow to the end of our friendship.

That was my first taste of what was to come. Nevertheless, I accepted his tantrum-filled reworking of our agreement and moved on. I was still selling properties and running my system. Oh, by the way, he didn't take over cash flow. We never saw him again at the cash flow event unless he came to say hi. But he took the teaching pay away, and that was really his goal.

Even those cuts weren't enough for Montenegro, so he got a bigger idea, a sinister idea. Money was everything to Montenegro. His identity was wrapped up in the money he made and in his own deep pockets. He started looking at all options.

The way our business arrangement worked is that each of the three partners shared in the profits: Geno was getting a cut, I was getting a cut, and Montenegro was the face of the company, and those were his students, so he was also getting a cut. At some point, he realized that if he completely cut me out of the business, he could keep my share all for himself.

That's what he decided to do. I wouldn't find out about his decision until months later.

AT SOME POINT, HE REALIZED THAT IF HE COMPLETELY CUT ME OUT OF THE BUSINESS, HE COULD KEEP MY SHARE ALL FOR HIMSELF.

THE MEDIA LOVES ME...NOT

In the middle of 2013, Montenegro made a big mistake. A major business magazine wanted to do an interview with him and write a piece about one of his big bus-tour training events. He was such an egomaniac he thought the reporter was going to write a glowing article about him. Montenegro showed off to the reporter the whole time, walking around the bus-tour event bragging and acting like a complete douchebag. The reporter just followed him around taking it all in. Montenegro thought the reporter was loving him and was impressed.

Instead, the magazine published a scathing article in which they called Montenegro a home-flipping huckster. The article basically called Montenegro a charlatan and a scammer. His reputation was already damaged, so when this hit piece came out, Montenegro's events turned into Death Valley. Hardly anyone showed up. The magazine article trashed his name. Along with all the other negative press, it hit him hard financially.

THE ARTICLE BASICALLY CALLED MONTENEGRO A CHARLATAN AND A SCAMMER.

It was a real low point for Montenegro and his company. You could tell in his demeanor that it was really affecting him. When Montenegro is losing money, his personality changes because everything is about money with him. It's the most important thing in his life. He basically began attacking everybody and everything around him. It was ugly. Nevertheless, I was loyal to Montenegro and Geno no matter what the property sales would be.

It was not lost on Montenegro that there was one part of the business that was doing great. It stuck out like a giant, blinking red light. It was my cash flow system I created. It was still very profitable and generating a lot of money.

STRANGE BEHAVIOR

After the magazine article came out in the middle of 2013, Montenegro started acting really funny. He became paranoid about my professional and personal relationship with Geno. Montenegro wasn't making money, and I think he was jealous because Geno and I were still making good money. This goes to Montenegro's leadership style. A bad leader doesn't want anyone to succeed anywhere. Montenegro liked to keep everyone else down; he always had to be the man on top. Again, let me be clear, this is business, and if Montenegro needed to cut ties and/or rework an agreement for the greater cause, then that is one thing. As a business owner, I fully understand that and don't blame him for that part.

After the magazine piece hit and Montenegro's financial struggles deepened, everything changed. He started acting strange. I sensed something was going on. Our relationship wasn't nearly as tight as it was before. He began holding me at arm's length.

Then something happened that changed everything. I took Geno's side in an argument he had with Montenegro. Montenegro got some inaccurate information about his funds that were tied up in some of our properties from his in-house paralegal. He was upset and became aggressive and belligerent with Geno over it on the phone. He insulted Geno and began yelling and screaming and hung up on him. Montenegro laid into Geno hard.

Geno called me right after, and he went nuts on the phone. He threatened to quit. He threatened to physically pound Montenegro into the earth. I spent an hour calming him down and putting him back together again. But enough was enough.

I called Montenegro to tell him he was wrong and Geno was right. Basically, I let Montenegro have it over the phone. I stuck up for Geno because Montenegro was way out of line. I had never done this before because I knew Montenegro had a fragile, childlike ego. This time, I had had it and just told him straight.

Well, Montenegro hates being told he's wrong. Looking back, I know my phone call enraged him. Not only that, but he got even more paranoid about my close relationship with Geno. I think Montenegro felt threatened by it. I think Montenegro used that phone call—and pure greed—as an excuse to do what he had been planning to do anyway.

As mentioned, Montenegro and I had been the closest of friends. We would probably talk ten times a day on the phone. We were as thick as thieves. But after that phone call, he was ice cold to me. No phone calls, nothing. When I asked him what was going on, he would say, "I just need to think. I don't want to talk about it right now." That was a massive message to me and the beginning of the end.

The weird part of this is that the two people who hated each other the most, Montenegro and Geno, somehow started talking more and getting closer after that incident. I noticed that Geno stopped trash-talking Montenegro to me like he used to do on a daily basis. That was so odd that it really stood out to me. I began to sense that they were forming some sort of alliance against me. I knew something was up, but I couldn't put my finger on what.

Let me rephrase that: I had an idea of what was up, but I thought, "Come on, there's no way two of my closest friends would do that to me." Wrong!

I THOUGHT, "COME ON, THERE'S NO WAY TWO OF MY CLOSEST FRIENDS WOULD DO THAT TO ME."

ICED OUT

Shortly after that phone call, one of my last events with Montenegro and Geno was a bus tour at the end of July 2013. By then, I could tell I was being circumvented. Montenegro completely ignored me. There was zero conversation. It was one of the worst times ever because I knew something was happening. At this point, I sensed what they were doing; I just didn't know to what extent and when it would happen.

I confronted Geno at that bus tour.

"What the fuck is going on?"

Geno told me that Montenegro approached him confidentially, but he wouldn't say about what. Geno just wouldn't be straight with me. I think Geno was feeling me out, trying to provide a soft landing for me without saying what was about to happen. He was giving bits and pieces because he was sworn to secrecy by Montenegro.

I pushed harder, demanding answers. Geno got defensive and even a little aggressive with me. He would not give me the facts. He wasn't being straight with me. His wife was there too, and she also refused to tell me anything. It became obvious that everyone was distancing themselves from me. They knew something I didn't. It was humiliating and infuriating. At that point, I knew I was out. This hurt me so deeply that it's hard to articulate in writing what I felt at that event.

THIS HURT ME SO DEEPLY THAT IT'S HARD TO ARTICULATE IN WRITING WHAT I FELT.

At that bus tour, I remember being emotionally messed up because two of my best friends were turning on me and were going to circumvent me. I knew they were screwing me over because no one would talk to me about it. I was so distraught that I had to go into my hotel room and deal with my emotions. I had to gather myself. It was a dark time.

But I had to be at the event. I had to do all the speaking that I do at the bus tour. I'll never forget going up on stage twice and just killing it. I blocked out all the pain and anger and focused on giving a great performance for the students. I told myself, "If I am going out, I am going out like a beast." From the outside looking in, you would never sense a thing was wrong. On the inside, I was gutted to my core. We sold twenty-eight properties that weekend at the bus tour. We had a great event. Even amid all that drama, it was still something that was really working.

After the bus tour, I was completely iced out. I couldn't get anyone to tell me what was going on. I felt distraught, traumatized, and abused. The next day, I had to leave for a business trip to Canada.

COLLECT CALL FROM EL DIABLO

Two weeks later, I had flown back up to Canada for a second time to run a real estate event where I was trying to get Canadian investors to attend a property tour in the United States. I had invested more than $100,000 to set up and market that event with Geno as my partner. I had fronted all the money, and our verbal agreement was that once we sold the properties, we were going to settle up, and Geno would pay me back his half. I had six figures of my own money on the line in Canada.

During my second trip to Canada for this NV (Nick Vertucci) and Geno event, I received the call. It was August 28, 2013. I answered.

Montenegro said, "Hey, you've been wanting to talk, so let's talk."

"OK," I said.

"Look, this is the bottom line. I am making a business decision right now and ending our business relationship."

"OK. Can you explain why to me?"

"I'm not going to go into the details, Nick," he said. "I know you're not going to have an easy time with it, so there's no sense in going around and around. It's over, and it's as simple as that."

"So you're making a business decision?"

"Yes. It doesn't mean our friendship has to be over. It's not personal," Montenegro replied.

"Well, it's fucking personal to me because I created this cash flow system and brought it into your company. I spent four and a half years working with you and being fiercely loyal to you, and all of a sudden, it's over, no explanation given. How is that not fucking personal? It's really fucking personal to me. And how does Geno fit into this decision? Let me guess: this means Geno has agreed to work with you directly?"

"Yes, I will be working with Geno directly from now on. I don't want to work with you anymore. Geno and I are going to be doing properties together."

"So you and Geno have conspired behind my back to basically take my business? How long has that been going on?"

"Look, Nick," he said. "I'm not going to argue the details with you. Here's the thing: you've had a good run. I bring in the students, Geno does a lot of the work on the ground, but I could have my salaried staff do what you do. You're just a broker in this deal. That's the way it is. I'm making a business decision."

"YOU'RE JUST A BROKER IN THIS DEAL."

Knowing him and his style, I said, "Let me guess," I said. "I can't even work with Geno if I want to continue to do my radio show or if I still want to provide properties and make a living."

"You know me well, Nick. Geno will be working with me exclusively."

"You're taking my whole business from me, the business that I created and built. If you do that and if Geno agreed to this, I can't even sell properties on the radio anymore. You have taken my legs out financially. I can't believe you are doing this to me."

"You'll be fine. You've created this before. You can reinvent it. You'll figure it out."

I said, "How do you live with yourself?"

"Listen, let me explain something to you," Montenegro said. "I care only about two things: I care about money, and I care about my three boys. I'll get back to you in what order. I have nothing more to say to you. If you want to still be friends, we can be friends."

"How the fuck can I be friends with you after what you just did to me?" I asked. "You're hurting my family. You're hurting my staff. You've just taken my business. You devalued me with this bullshit comment that I'm just a broker. I created this system. The reason you have no complaints is because of me, not because of Geno. So whether you know it or not, you're making a huge mistake."

"I don't believe so," he said. "And there's nothing further to talk about."

We hung up, and that was it. I was crushed. He was one of my closest friends. Geno was one of my closest friends too. We were tight, all of us, and so were our wives. How could this be real?

Montenegro apparently thought he would be just fine without me: he could teach my cash flow course, he could do the speaking on stage, he could have his staff sell the properties, and he could just plug his people into the positions where all my staff and I were. What really stung me was that Geno did not come to me and tell me that any of these conversations were taking place. How could he do this to me? How could he agree to cut me out?

As soon as I pulled myself together, I picked up the phone and called Geno. He answered. I said to him, "I just talked to Montenegro. I can't believe this happened. Are you serious, that he just called me and told me this?"

Geno said, "Nick, listen. This is a fucked-up situation. I just moved to Orlando. I have employees. I didn't know what to do."

"How about my fucking employees, man?"

Two years later, Geno admitted to me he made this decision out of fear. I found out later how Montenegro threatened him. Apparently, Montenegro went to Geno at that last bus tour and pulled Geno and his wife, Elana, into a room.

He said, "You have a choice to make. You can work with me directly and I'll pay you more per property than you're making now, but the rest of Nick's cut goes to me. If not, then you're out too. Decide now. Either way, Nick's out."

I know Geno's wife pushed him to do it because they

had moved from Las Vegas to Orlando. They had the infrastructure that we had built together, so it was a pure greed grab on both sides, plus a lot of fear on Geno and Elana's side as well. By cutting me out, they would both make more money. Geno's wife was the decision maker on most things, so she probably pushed him to make this decision too.

Geno should not have done that to me. He should have had the balls to stand up for me. He and I had many conversations about being friends and always having each other's back no matter what. I desperately want to believe that Geno struggled with the decision to stab me in the back because he didn't want to risk losing everything. The fear of losing everything got to him. Geno apparently didn't have as big a set of balls as he always told me he did. When the chips are down, you really learn who has big balls and who doesn't. Geno didn't.

Regardless of his reasons, he did it to me. He did it to my family. I had worked so hard for years to build a massive cash flow engine, and for what? To have it taken away by two people I thought were my friends—one I brought the properties to and one I brought into my system. After four and a half years together, they both turned on me and left me twisting in the wind with nothing.

AFTER FOUR AND A HALF YEARS TOGETHER, THEY BOTH TURNED ON ME AND LEFT ME TWISTING IN THE WIND WITH NOTHING.

LOWEST OF LOWS

It was the lowest point in my life. I was devastated. I was in Canada, alone, away from my family and support system, and I was absolutely leveled.

Both of my close friends had plotted behind my back and betrayed me. I had no business model left. I had to cancel the event I was at in Canada because I no longer had any properties to provide since I was no longer allowed to work with Geno. The $100,000 investment I had put into that event was wasted and worthless. I had to refund everyone's money. It was a disaster.

I came back home and informed my office staff of what happened. I didn't know what I was going to do with them. I didn't know what my next step was, but I decided to pay them through December. I didn't want them to worry about anything, though I was up front with them about what happened.

I said, "I don't know what's going to happen. Stick with me until December so you don't have to worry about the holidays. If I decide I'm gone, then you will all have to figure out what to do next, but I'll let you know before December."

Then I disappeared for a few weeks. I was so emotionally leveled by the betrayal and the rejection that I was physically weak. I lost my edge. I lost my mojo. I honestly had to peel myself out of bed each day for the first couple of weeks. I sank into depression and didn't know what I was going to do. All my sweat equity, my livelihood, my closest friends, and my identity were gone just like that.

To add insult to injury, Montenegro was telling everyone at the company that I didn't bring anything to the table that was worth keeping around. If Montenegro has a special gift, it's devaluing people. I saw it constantly when we worked together. He devalues the worth and contribution of others and overvalues his own worth and contribution. Montenegro thought the cash flow business wouldn't skip a beat after stealing it from me and forcing me out. I think what eventually happened surprised everyone, even me.

MONTENEGRO THOUGHT THE CASH FLOW BUSINESS WOULDN'T SKIP A BEAT AFTER STEALING IT FROM ME AND FORCING ME OUT.

MILLIONS HELD HOSTAGE

Unlike when I lost the computer business, this time I was

OK financially because I had built up my financial intelligence and made wise use of my money. The problem was that most of my capital was tied up in our system, in properties under Geno's control.

I didn't have the business structured properly, so Montenegro was able to strong-arm Geno. He told Geno, "You will not release any funds to Nick. I don't care if the money is his or not. Don't release any money until I have a signed dissolution agreement in place with him." Geno wanted to protect his golden egg, so he agreed.

Because I had only a verbal agreement with Geno, I had a very difficult time getting my money. It took me months. I'll explain why later. So not only did Geno not have my back, but he also kept my money. Fear and weakness are revealed during the darkest of times.

SALT IN THE WOUND

Montenegro wanted me to sign this onerous, one-sided agreement that exempted him from any liability. He knew he had stolen my business and my business relationship. The legal term is tortious interference, also known as intentional interference. It was a bully tactic, but what could I do? I had no access to my own capital. It was tied up, and Geno refused to release it to me because of Montenegro's iron fist.

In the weeks after this went down, I wasn't even fighting for the money or my dignity because I wasn't in fight mode yet. I felt utterly dismantled and destroyed. What happened over the next few weeks was truly bizarre, and it doesn't make sense to anyone.

Montenegro would make people who worked for him, my former peers and friends, text me from events. They would send me taunting messages that said things like, "Hey, you're on stage in fifteen minutes. Where are you? Oops. Oh, I forgot. You're not here at the event." They were cruelly mocking me for Montenegro's entertainment.

I often talked about the book *Who Moved My Cheese?* on stage, so Montenegro photoshopped my face onto the book cover and changed the title to *Who Moved My Cash Flow Business?* and sent it to me via text message. Actually, he had someone else do it because he was too big of a pussy to do it himself. He was deliberately taunting me. It was bizarre because we'd been the best of friends, but that's the way he operated. Once he turned on someone, he became vicious.

I'd seen him do this sort of thing to other people, and unfortunately, I'd always turned a blind eye to it. He could be aggressive with anyone. I had looked the other way for a long time because I was making a lot of money. I would justify it by telling myself he had never treated me like that, but it was just an excuse because of the money I was making. Honestly, he's the biggest moron on the planet, so shame on me for getting close to someone like that.

The mocking texts continued regularly for weeks. I didn't even fight back. My jaw was on the ground. I couldn't believe it. I was devastated. On top of that, I was trying to fight for my money.

I was surprised by how many of my former coworkers and friends turned their backs on me. I had a lot of close friendships in Montenegro's organization. The sad part is that you find out through adversity who your friends really are and who was never really a friend. Almost all of them turned their backs on me when the chips were down. Let me correct that: all of them did. Emphasis on *all of them*.

Finally, after a few weeks, I began to come out of my deep depression. I decided to try to reinvent the cash flow operation that I had originally created. I knew Houston was a good cash flow market at the time, so I decided to give it a try. I started making calls, flying out there, meeting people, and trying to build an infrastructure. I was trying to re-create the wheel I had built many times before.

I was also looking for a place to sell the properties, so I contacted a guy I knew named Scott Bell. Scott was a friend of mine whom I'd provided properties for in the past. He was a real estate training promoter, and although he did things the old-fashioned way, he knew how to promote. I began providing him about twenty properties from my beginning efforts in Houston.

THAT'S IT. I AM OUT

It didn't take long for me to notice the situation in Houston didn't feel right. I couldn't put my finger on why. I just didn't want to do it. I didn't know if I was working with the wrong team or if I just had no passion for it anymore. Like I said, I lost my mojo. I didn't feel like getting up in the morning and running the business.

I didn't even care if I succeeded in Houston. All I knew was my heart wasn't in it. I didn't feel confident in the infrastructure I was building there, and I was worried I'd end up with egg on my face because of it. I didn't even have the desire to fix it or find somebody else to work with.

I decided to cut ties in Houston. I called Scott Bell because he already knew what I was going through. I said, "Dude, I'm out. I can't provide you any more properties for your events. I don't have the right infrastructure, and I don't think I can do you right. I'm pasting this thing together just to try to hustle up properties, and I actually don't want to do it. I don't know why."

Scott was very gracious about it. He said, "Thank you for leveling with me, Nick. I totally get it. I'd rather you not provide me properties that you can't stand behind. I appreciate your honesty. I'll figure out the property stuff."

Through our conversations, Scott was aware of what happened between me and Montenegro. "I can't believe that guy did you dirty like that," Scott said. "Nick, I just have one question for you. Why don't you start your own training company?"

"What? How? Scott, I have no idea how to run a training company. I don't have a TV show. I have no platform. Who am I?" I had never run my own training company. I didn't know the first thing about getting something like that off the ground.

"I don't think you need a TV show," Scott said. "You're the real deal. You invest in real estate. A lot of these guys on these seminar banners don't even do that. I'm a promoter. I could help you. I'll be a consultant and help you promote the training while you build the curriculum. You could create whatever kind of training you want and provide properties. You'd be great at it. You're a great communicator."

"I don't know, man. My money is all tied up. I'm leveled emotionally. You know, Scott, let me just think about it. But I doubt it."

IT HIT ME LIKE A TON OF BRICKS

I started thinking about it. For a week or two, I just started marinating on it. I was in limbo. That's when it finally dawned on me. The reason I couldn't go back into the cash flow business was because what I had come to love was working with students. Teaching, providing properties to show them how to do it right, how to protect their interests, and all the other stuff that I had been doing at the live events through Montenegro's company.

That's what I missed doing. When I finally saw all of this clearly, I thought, "This is what I should be doing. This is what I love." It hit me like a ton of bricks.

I called Scott Bell back and said, "I'm in. I don't know how, but fuck it. Let's do this."

In mid-October, he and I made a short-term agreement so he could help me launch. He said, "Nick, you need to launch in January. That's the busiest time in this industry."

When I tell you I worked morning, noon, and night putting the new business together, it's an understatement. I learned as I went, getting the curriculum written, creating all the student training materials, designing internal processes, developing marketing and advertising, and trying to hire people so I could have maybe one team out on the road for live events.

A few people came over from the old company, the few who were loyal to me and wanted to give the new company a try. Let me be clear: these were people who either had quit or were fired from Montenegro's evil empire. Everyone else refused because they didn't think it was going to work. We were launching a new venture, and they didn't want to take a chance. To be fair, the risks were high. Most new real estate training companies go out of business within a few months or less, because launching takes a lot of cash up front, or they don't have the right message or marketing or training curriculum. Many don't even try. It's not for the faint of heart due to big up-front costs and a low success rate.

WARRIOR MODE

Even though I was afraid that I could lose a bunch of money and fail, I persisted. The magnitude of this undertaking was so immense. I knew failure was possible, but I was determined not to let Montenegro or Geno say, "See? You really are just a broker. We told you that you can't succeed without us." Because I was so down, that negative thought set in my mind. I lost confidence, and I had lost my identity. To push forward, I knew I had to revert back to tapping into my biggest asset—my mind—and go into warrior mode.

I was determined not to fail, to prove them wrong, to

prove that I was not just a broker. So I didn't give that fear a chance to overcome me. Instead, I took it by the horns and beast-moded it away. I would drive around in my car and repeat to myself, "Bullshit! I am the best in this business." I would say it out loud constantly. I said it to myself anytime the fear and doubt came over me.

Think about this: I was yelling, "Bullshit! I am the best in this business," and I didn't even have the corporation set up or the name of my company yet. But I was determined for that thought pattern to become reality. I decided I would die trying if I had to, but it was going to happen.

I self-talked my way through it and built myself back up. I envisioned this company that didn't even have a name yet, and I convinced myself it would succeed. If you'd been sitting next to me in a car, you would have thought I was some crazy guy yelling, "Bullshit! I am the best in this business!" over and over and over. But I didn't care what anyone else thought.

I had no choice because I was fighting for my life, fighting to recover my money, and fighting not to sign that one-sided agreement with Montenegro. I had to leverage my home to the tune of $800,000 to start the business because Montenegro and Geno wouldn't release my liquid cash that was tied up in those properties, and my other assets were tied up in real estate. It's difficult to launch a new business under the best of circumstances, let alone when dealing with the monumental obstacles that I was facing. The stress and pressure were almost unbearable.

I WILL DISMANTLE YOU

I knew Montenegro would push back. I knew he would come after me. I didn't know how or when, but I knew his style, and I had seen him do it to other people. He didn't want anyone else invading his space, so he freely sued competitors and former employees.

His employees were afraid to leave. Nobody wanted to quit and work somewhere else because they were deathly afraid of Montenegro. They knew he would sue you to the point of devastation if you didn't have deep pockets to fight back. He had this hold on everyone. It was his signature leadership style. He led from a place of fear.

Montenegro called me at one point in the middle of all of this, around November 2013, when he caught wind that I was launching a training company. Without letting me speak, he said, "If you come after any of my people, if you even talk to one person who works for me, I will fucking dismantle you. I will legally and financially dismantle you. So crawl back under the rock I found you under." Then he hung up on me.

I looked at the phone and thought, "Nice chat," and went about my business.

"I WILL LEGALLY AND FINANCIALLY DISMANTLE YOU. SO CRAWL BACK UNDER THE ROCK I FOUND YOU UNDER."

LEARNING CURVES AHEAD

I didn't know what I was doing in the training business. I was trying to figure it out as I did it. All day, every day, I grinded to start this business. Somehow, I managed to launch in January. I don't even know how it happened. That's why I say it seemed like it happened with fairy dust or a magic wand. I don't know how I did it, except to say I willed it into existence and worked my fuckin' ass off.

When students registered, I didn't know what to do. That's how green I was. I took Scott Bell up on his offer of being a consultant for my new business. He helped me with some of the moving parts, but I still had to learn on the ground. Another thing I tell my students is that it doesn't matter how much advice or information someone gives you. You still have to learn any business on the ground by just doing it. You have to learn by actually doing it and putting tread on your tires.

IT DOESN'T MATTER HOW MUCH ADVICE OR INFORMATION SOMEONE GIVES YOU. YOU STILL HAVE TO LEARN ANY BUSINESS ON THE GROUND BY JUST DOING IT.

I remember thinking, "There's no way people are going to call and register for my event." But they started calling and registering. Then I thought, "There's no way they're actually going to show up." Then they showed up. From the beginning, we had wild success.

I don't know if it was divine intervention or simply hard work or both, but I had solid traction right away. My first three-day workshop event was in Washington, DC. People had already shown up to the free presentation. Then out of that free presentation, about fifty people signed up for my first three-day paid workshop event, and each of them could bring a guest. Altogether, about one hundred people came to the paid three-day event, which is considered a big success in this industry. I was thrilled.

SERVED UP HOT

That event in DC was also the first Montenegro sighting. I had refused to sign the one-sided agreement he was trying to force down my throat. And I was still fighting for my money.

During the event, one of my main guys, Jamie, called me

and said, "Hey, we just caught this guy at the door. He's a process server."

A court process server? Unbelievable. Montenegro deliberately sent someone to serve me a lawsuit while I was on stage at my first big training event. It was a petty and vindictive attempt to embarrass me and derail my new company before it even got off the ground.

I wasn't at the event when Montenegro's process server showed up. Montenegro thought I would be, so Jamie read the papers to me over the phone. Montenegro was suing me for starting my own business in the industry that he thought he owned. It said right there on the cover page of instructions for the server, "If he's on stage, hand it to him on stage. Embarrass him. What's his reaction?" Montenegro had written a long list of crazy instructions designed to kill my event and destroy my students' trust in me and my company.

If the students had seen me getting sued, they would think the worst and would not work with me. Pretty low, but I've seen this behavior before from Montenegro. Here's an example. One of his free-preview speakers had enough of his shit and quit. So Montenegro would send out some random hired female actor to stand up in the middle of the two-hour class and yell, "You got me pregnant." It was an awful way to discredit the speaker and blow up the class. Montenegro had no low he wouldn't sink to. This was who I was fighting.

At the DC event, even the process server said, "Is he crazy? I've never had a request like this before." Montenegro instructed the server to take a head count. Montenegro was curious because I'd launched my competing business, and he felt threatened.

The server said to Jamie, "Listen, I don't really want to do this. Can I just take a head count and hand you the papers?"

Jamie had to convince him I wasn't there because I wasn't there. I spoke on the phone with the guy and said, "I'm in California. You're not going to ruin my event."

"I have no interest in doing that. Can I please just take a head count?"

I thought, "Yeah, sure, do it. Because I have a hundred people in there." I knew when Montenegro heard that, it would be one of the biggest tacos he ever had to swallow. I was hoping he would choke on it.

I said, "My guy will let you take a look. You're going to take your head count. But if you interrupt the event or say one word, he's going to choke you out." And Jamie was the type to do it.

The server said, "Don't threaten me."

I said, "Too late, I just did. Do you want the head count or not?"

He took the head count, and he left. Then my attorneys called and accepted service on my behalf.

FEEL THIS

Montenegro circumvented me and took my cash flow business and was now suing me and trying to take my new business. He was refusing to release my money unless I signed a one-sided agreement. He had been mocking me, and he had been threatening me. Three days later, after we took service, I was walking up to my door when this lady approached me from her car.

"Hey, Nick," she said. "You've been served."

"I was already served."

"I know," she said. "He wanted me to tell you that he just wanted you to feel it."

"OK, great," I said. "Tell him I said, 'Feel this!'" I asked to take a selfie with her, but she refused and left. You just can't make this stuff up!

SUE THEM ALL

Apparently suing me wasn't enough for Montenegro. Next, he started suing as many of my employees as he could. He wanted to put pressure on them. He wanted to send a message to them and to the entire industry that anyone who works for me would pay a steep price. He was trying to destroy my business.

As one example, he was suing people who made $30,000 a year who had not worked for him for the past year or two. He was suing people he had fired. You can't do that under the law, but he did it anyway. You see, the strategy was to just sue and make them spend money until he got his way. Unfortunately, our legal system isn't perfect, and that was an effective strategy.

He wanted the word to get out that anyone who went to work for me would face thousands of dollars in legal fees. This was a tactic he employed often. He would bully and demoralize people into submission with baseless legal actions that he knew had no merit but would cause innocent people fear, worry, and expense. Most of the time, unfortunately, this worked.

He told everyone in his company, "If you leave here and go work for Vertucci, I will sue you." Word would always get back to me what he said in his meetings. "If you go work for Vertucci, I will dismantle you financially and every single person in your family." People were afraid to come work with me because they didn't want to incur his wrath. Most people just couldn't handle that type of pressure. When you lead from a place of fear with an iron fist, you don't create loyalty.

I took on the lower-income employees' lawsuits so they didn't have to pay for their own legal defense. I took on the expenses and fought for them in court. I wanted people to know that if they took the risk to work for me, I would have their back.

Meanwhile, I had to lock down all of my events with extra expense for security because he was trying to serve everybody. He wanted to blow up my events and create fear with the students so they wouldn't purchase anything from me.

When I did my first bus tour in 2014, a major event that was critical to the success of my business, of course he sent a server. He tried to serve two or three people there. But I was used to it by then. We took service, but we didn't let him disrupt the event.

That first bus tour went great. We had an incredible turn-out, a promising start to the year, and the business was succeeding. All my hard work and the risks I took were beginning to pay off.

AN OFFER YOU CAN'T REFUSE

Around this time, right after that first bus tour in March 2014, my mother passed away. She'd been in hospice for a while, and she finally passed. Montenegro found out about this, so he messaged me on Facebook. He saw his opening.

The message said, "Hey, I heard about your mother. I did want to send my condolences. We were close friends, and this probably doesn't need to go any further. We should chat."

"Wait a minute," I said to myself. "This guy fucking took my business. He's been mocking me. He's trying to dismantle my new business and attack me and everyone in my company, but we should talk now because we're friends. Really?"

But I agreed to it because I was curious what he'd have to say. I said OK, and we set up a time to talk. I sat in my truck so I would be alone, and we called each other. After a minute of insincere condolences, he got to his "amazing" offer for me.

He said, "This doesn't have to go any further, but here's the deal. You know, we were the best of friends at one point, so I'm going to propose something to you." He used some dumb analogy about Apple and Microsoft being rivals but learning to work together. Then he said,

"I have two proposals for you, OK? I want you to really think about them."

"OK, what's the first one?"

"Here it is," he said. "You keep whoever you have right now, and anytime you want to hire someone, you hire someone from outside the industry or you talk to me about it."

"So you want me to ask your permission to hire somebody? Even if it's somebody who worked for you years ago?"

"Well, Nick, I know your personality, and I know what you're thinking. But I just want you to consider it, because we can work together. I know a lot about this business. Maybe I can even help."

I felt like saying, "Fuck you. You ran your company into the ground, you dope. Why would I want your advice?"

That's the first time it dawned on me that he feared me. He feared that everyone was going to want to work for me. He feared that I was going to have massive success.

I said, "What's the second proposal? Because I'm not crazy about the first one."

"Well, you're going to like the second one even less."

"Well, what is it?"

"You go out of business."

"So my two choices are to ask for your permission before I hire someone or I go out of business?"

"Nick, I want you to take your time, and you better think about it, because whether you realize it or not, you are making a seven-figure decision right now."

"YOU ARE MAKING A SEVEN-FIGURE DECISION RIGHT NOW."

That statement hit me profoundly. I'll explain why in a moment. I said, "Listen, I will never ask your permission for anything, and I'm not going anywhere."

"Then, Nick, I'm going to fucking dismantle you."

"Well, we'll see about that. I'll see you in the end zone, then." We hung up.

Montenegro had already stripped me of my identity and took my cash flow business, and now he was trying for the second time to hurt me and my family. He had come after me personally, cut me to my core, and now he was attacking me again. He took my business from me the first time, and now he wanted another pound of flesh.

SEVEN-FIGURE DECISION

When Montenegro told me I was making a "seven-figure decision," that phrase had a profound impact on me. It was like time stopped. After we hung up, I just sat there. It felt like a surreal moment, and I wasn't entirely sure why. But it dawned on me soon after.

My entire life has been a series of seven-figure decisions. Your life is a series of seven-figure decisions. Seven-figure decisions are so powerful that they truly determine the quality of our lives and the lives of our families. It's why I chose that phrase as the title of this book.

I began thinking back through my life. When I chose not to go to college, that was a seven-figure decision. When I took $25,000 and invested it into the computer business, that was a seven-figure decision. When I chose to go to that three-day real estate course, that was a seven-figure decision. When I demanded mentorship, that was a seven-figure decision. Each of our lives is made up of seven-figure decisions.

I didn't even realize that my decision making was such a game of inches and that it got me where I am today. When Montenegro said that to me, it was so profound. I don't even think Montenegro knew how profound it was. That's why you're reading this book titled *Seven-Figure Decisions*. For him, it was just a bullying tactic; for me, it was a life-changing moment that has fueled my massive success. It was a moment that was going to define who I was.

IT WAS A MOMENT THAT WAS GOING TO DEFINE WHO I WAS.

DEATH THREATS

At my next bus tour event, one of Montenegro's servers was tossed out a little harder than he liked. The next day, the server called my hotel room and threatened my wife and children. He said, "You fucked up. You're all fucking dead." We filed a police report. The police contacted Montenegro because he'd sent the server. Of course, he denied it. But I was in 100 percent beast mode now. You can try to hurt me, but if you try to hurt my loved ones, you have made the worst mistake of your life. That was the only time I texted him during this. I cannot even write in this book what I wrote, but I meant every word of it.

Because of Montenegro's threats and because of the gut-wrenching stuff he did to me, I had such a fire building inside me. I built my new company and used his actions and words as rocket fuel. He's probably why and how I built my company so big and so fast. I had such fierce motivation to win in this business because of the obstacles this fucker was throwing at me. Not to mention, this was my destiny, and nobody was going to get in the way. Nobody.

Now I had a decision to make, a big decision, because it was going to cost me a lot of money. My business was brand new. I had many people around me telling me to make concessions and settle the lawsuit. "Make a deal, Nick. You don't need this. It's too much negativity. Just let it go and move on. Sign some sort of agreement and settlement."

As I say elsewhere in this book, sometimes standing on principle is not the way to go, and you have to consider the long term. But this was different. This was a defining moment for me and my business.

THIS WAS A DEFINING MOMENT FOR ME AND MY BUSINESS.

MY BIGGEST SEVEN-FIGURE DECISION

I decided I was going to take a stand. I knew that I would never look at myself the same way again if I submitted to this threat. I thought, "I will live in a cardboard box before I succumb to this. If I cave in to this dick, I will never be able to look at myself in the mirror. I am going to fight him with everything I have."

When Montenegro said I had a seven-figure decision to make, he was trying to intimidate me and get me to cave in. But it backfired on him because that statement is what locked me in and made me 100 percent determined to fight him with every ounce of strength I had.

I knew this truly was a seven-figure decision. I was either going to be great at the end of it, or I was going to be destroyed and have to tuck my tail between my legs and crawl into a hole. If I had caved in and signed those papers and agreed to his conditions, you would not be reading this book today. Not only that, but thousands of my students would not be where they are today; they would not have their success in real estate.

Please understand that I'm not telling you to stand on principle every time you have a conflict. On the contrary, it often makes more sense to make a quick, inexpensive decision not to fight someone in order to protect your reputation and time—even when you know you're right and the other person is flat-out wrong. Avoiding a fight is the wise move most of the time. Not to mention, I have an extremely long fuse and can generally absorb a lot, until the point I have no choice but to fight.

But when your very identity, your livelihood, your honor, and your personal integrity—not to mention millions of dollars— are at stake, you have no choice but to dig your heels in and fight. There is a big difference between those two scenarios, and you have to decide for yourself what that difference is for you. It was crystal clear to me that I had to fight.

FLASHBACK TO CHILDHOOD

I learned this lesson early in life. As mentioned earlier, my father was my original mentor and role model. He taught me something very valuable when I was eight years old. After every baseball game, all the teams would gather at the snack shop for some postgame treats. One of my all-time favorites was the Chili Billie, which was tortilla chips, chili, and cheese. But an ongoing issue was starting to occur. This one kid from another team began to see me as a target for some reason. For a few weeks in a row, he would do things such as try to knock the food out of my hand or throw something in my food. I would shrug it off and do my best to avoid the situation. He was much bigger than I was, and I wanted no part of him. I had looked my dad's way a couple times and got zero reaction from him. I was thinking, "Hey, Dad, a little help here?"

One day, walking to the car, I said, "Dad, can you tell that kid to leave me alone?"

He said, "Nicky [that was what my family called me], I won't be here to fight your battles for you forever. If you want that kid to stop, you have to take a stand. It may not go your way, but that's how it will stop, and that's how you can be sure nobody else will start that behavior with you."

It was not at all what I wanted to hear. I was stunned. Was my dad telling me to fight?

The next week came, and again I was caught between the excitement of getting that Chili Billie and the pressure of this damn kid bothering me. True to form, the kid tossed a baseball at my hands to knock the food from my hand. He missed. I looked at my dad, who just looked at me and kind of pursed his lips and shrugged his shoulders with the look of "It's your problem, not mine, buddy."

I remember having a huge knot in my stomach from fear and thinking out what I was going to do. It seemed like an eternity while I decided. Then, all at once, I just thought, "Fuck it." I dropped my coveted Chili Billie and ran and tackled that kid and started hitting him with all my puny arms had. After maybe just ten seconds, I felt my body rise from the ground. My dad had lifted me off him. Apparently, a full beating wasn't my dad's plan.

The kid was yelling, "OK, OK, stop! Stop!"

The kid's father ran over and was yelling, "What the hell is going on?"

My dad looked at him said, "He had it coming," and we walked away.

On the way to the car, Dad put his hand on my head and said, "You did what you had to do. Sometimes you have no choice. Good job."

No more words were spoken, but I tell you, I never forgot those words. Not to mention, I felt like the featherweight champ of the world at that moment.

THE WHEELS OF JUSTICE TURN SLOW

For two and a half years, I fought him in the courts. I moved the case from Texas to California and from state court to federal court, where you're not allowed to discover people to death so you can try to keep costs down. There was also another benefit. His in-house, salaried attorneys were experienced in state court, but they didn't know how to win in federal court. So now he had to hire an outside law firm. That meant he was now paying his legal team by the hour, which started costing him real money. This changed the dynamic of the case and put him on his heels. Also, moving from Texas in-state court to California federal court was also a huge loss for him.

His in-house attorneys were hacks. They had limited skills and experience. They were accustomed to taking lawsuits only so far because most of their victims would settle early on to avoid the expense of a long, drawn-out legal battle. They had no experience in seeing a legal case all the way through to the end. When the case got real, they were in over their heads. They were hacks working for food.

He wasn't prepared for my tenacity or for my counterambush. What he didn't realize is that he tortiously interfered with my original cash flow business with Geno. That means he was legally liable for the damage he caused me. I countersued him for $10 million.

I COUNTERSUED HIM FOR $10 MILLION.

He wasn't expecting me to punch back like that. Most people whom he sued just gave in to him rather than getting into a legal battle. When I countersued Montenegro, now he was the one who had to make a seven-figure decision.

It was never my intention to sue Montenegro. After he circumvented me, I had planned to just take my ball and go home. I was going to chalk it up to experience and move on. But then he sued me out of spite, bravado, ego, fear, and insecurity. I had to defend myself. When you're a defendant in a legal court battle for your life and livelihood, all lawful options are on the table. That's why I sued him. He has only himself to blame.

At first, he wanted me to pay him money and agree to his demands in order to end the lawsuit. But I dug in so hard and fought so fiercely that he finally accepted he wasn't going to break me. And trust me, he tried everything, and I mean everything. As the tables turned and I went on the offensive, he realized he was going to lose.

Three times during the two-and-a-half-year legal battle, the judge mandated that we attend mediations and attempt to settle the suit. Each time, Montenegro asked for a walkaway. He said he was willing to drop the suit. I wouldn't budge. Too late. At that point, he realized that he'd stepped into something that he could not get out of.

"NOW YOUSE CAN'T LEAVE"

When Montenegro went from aggressively suing me to wishing he never had, it reminded me of that famous bar scene in the movie *A Bronx Tale*. It begins when a motorcycle gang roars into a small New York Italian town. Then the burly gang members enter a local bar and start getting rowdy and disrespectful—not knowing the bar is run by the mob. The mob boss, a well-dressed gentleman in a suit, politely asks the gang members to leave. They refuse. So the mob boss walks over to the front door of the bar, takes out his keys, and locks the door. He turns around and says to the gang, "Now youse can't leave." In that moment, the gang members realized they had made a fatal mistake. What happens next? Well, you can watch it on YouTube. Let's just say the bikers wish they had never started trouble in the first place. A lesson learned the hard way.

The nerve of that guy to ask me for a walkaway after putting me through two and a half years of hell. After he threatened my family. After he took my first business away. After he tried to destroy my second business. After he tried to disrupt my live events. After he forced me to spend a ton of time, money, and energy fighting him. After he tried suing my employees. After he tried to tear my family apart with dirty tactics. After all that, when he sees he's going to lose, then he wants to walk away? Well, guess what? Now youse can't leave.

I went hard after him. The harder I fought, the more I trained my mind, and the more I dug in, the more he realized I wasn't giving in. Many people and my attorneys told me to not take an aggressive posture.

At first, he fought me on social media, insulting me without using my name. It was almost comical, but I had to fight back.

Everyone said to me, "Hey, man, why are you poking the bear?"

When I responded to him on social media, I didn't use his name either, but he knew. We were both so obvious. I kept pounding the hell out of him. People in the industry knew this was going on, and they sent our posts back and forth, saying, "Ooh, look what happened today. Look at what Vertucci said today."

My attorneys even told me to mellow out. I told them, "Listen, you guys don't understand. You guys want to be politicians, but I know this asshole feeds on weakness. I'm never going to show weakness. So you guys do your job. I'll do mine."

HIS SECRET BAT PHONE

Things started going my way. I finally received my money that was being held by Geno. He tapped out once I put legal pressure on him. He finally said, "Screw this," and he paid me in full. I had the leg up on him legally because I had legitimate legal claims to that money. He had none. He was afraid I would sue him. I believe that Geno never really wanted to hold my money hostage. He was doing what Montenegro told him to do because he was afraid of losing what he had.

I knew there was a risk that I could lose the case if it went to trial. Juries are unpredictable. There was tremendous personal pressure on me to walk away. I just couldn't. There was no way I was walking away at that point. I was going to finish this.

THERE WAS TREMENDOUS PERSONAL PRESSURE ON ME TO WALK AWAY. I JUST COULDN'T. THERE WAS NO WAY I WAS WALKING AWAY AT THAT POINT. I WAS GOING TO FINISH THIS.

Montenegro even made secret phone calls to me himself,

trying to get me to settle. He called me from a private number because he wasn't supposed to contact me directly. "Hey, Nick, this is Taco." He tried to convince me to walk away by appealing to our friendship. That was laughable. He destroyed the friendship the moment he circumvented me.

He was just trying to manipulate me because he knew he was going to lose in court. He said he wanted us both to walk away, but what he really wanted was for his liability to go away. If he had me by the throat, he would for sure have finished me off. But he didn't, and he knew it. He even wanted to talk numbers, what it would take for me to drop the lawsuit. He was showing his weakness. I knew it was not easy for him to make those calls.

At one point, he said, "I'll allow you to work with Geno again."

That ploy struck me as particularly pathetic and hysterical because Montenegro had no control over me, and Geno already contacted me about wanting to work with me again.

Montenegro even said, "Maybe we can start buying media together to save us both money."

I almost laughed out loud at that one. As if I would ever work with him again. Give me a break. Not a chance.

I knew that settling was the smart thing to do. But this was a two-and-a-half-year legal battle of sweat, blood, and guts. He hit me with every dirty trick in the book, and I survived them all. Even though it would have been much easier—and way cheaper—for me to walk away, I just couldn't do it. I had to see it through. I had to finish it.

Plus, Montenegro has done this to so many people. He used his in-house hack attorneys to intimidate and crush people who didn't have the resources to fight back. I had to stand up to him and finish this for them as well. All the dirty tactics he thought would bring me to my knees did not. That's when he started to panic. I was determined to give him a taste of his own medicine.

Three weeks or so prior to the trial, his attorneys asked my attorney, "What is it going to take to make this go away?" They did not want to go to trial, because they believed they were going to lose.

I told my attorney, Madison, "You tell them this, and if you don't say this exactly as I'm saying it, I'm going to be furious. You tell them, 'If your client wants out of this, then, well, I guess he has a seven-figure decision to make.'"

"IF YOUR CLIENT WANTS OUT OF THIS, THEN, WELL, I GUESS HE HAS A SEVEN-FIGURE DECISION TO MAKE."

And can you believe that was that? He caved and settled. That was it. He had had enough. When I got the news, I just sat there. A rush of emotions came over me that I had been carrying and repressing for a long time. What I remember was that defining moment when I had that decision to make. Yes, that seven-figure decision during the call with Montenegro. I swear I heard the words spoken to me by my father, "Nicky, you did what you had to do. Good job." It was a surreal moment.

I can't disclose how much we settled for, but I put it behind me. His business is still on the morphine drip, barely limping along, or maybe he is gone by now. I really don't know. He is the most irrelevant person on the planet to me and to this industry. He's a nothing burger! And as a final sign of my complete vindication over him, almost every single person who ever worked for him works for me now.

When I first began working with Montenegro, he was a bigger-than-life character. He was brash and bold and intimidating. People shuddered at the thought of his attack. People feared him. That's how fear works. Your fears become what you make of them, and they'll grow as big as you let them. Of course, there are things you should legitimately be afraid of, things that can truly harm you, but we give fear more power than it deserves.

By the end of the lawsuit, I saw him for what he really

was—an insecure, frightened, small person who tries to bully and belittle people so no one would see through him. In a way, Montenegro reminded me of *The Wizard of Oz*. Everyone was frightened of the all-powerful Oz. But then his curtain was peeled away, and people saw the real him. As Montenegro's empire crumbled and his lawsuit unraveled, everyone saw him for what he truly was—a sad, little person (well, not little—he's humungous actually, but you know what I mean) who inflated his own ego and belittled others as a way to mask his own insecurity.

When I realized what he really was, I pitied him.

WHEN I REALIZED WHAT HE REALLY WAS, I PITIED HIM.

DON'T CREATE YOUR OWN COMPETITION, DUMMY

What he feared, he created. Montenegro had my complete loyalty for years, but he betrayed me. In so doing, he created his biggest competitor. He stopped working with Geno not long after the settlement because there were so many complaints against the company. Montenegro kept Geno in his company so he could use him against me as a witness in the case. As soon as Montenegro didn't need him anymore, Geno was out.

They didn't understand what it took to run my end of the

business. They didn't know how to treat clients. With no integrity, no heart, and no foundation, they sold properties to students. They didn't care about the students. The negative press piled up, and their sales started unwinding. Their whole system fell apart. For every three properties sold, two would unwind.

Geno and Montenegro had their own unique talents. Geno knew how to buy and manage properties. Like I said, he was and is a very talented real estate investor. I have a lot of respect for him in that area. Montenegro could be charismatic and endearing when he wanted to be, but his ego and greed could not be contained. And deep down, he has a very dark soul that can't be hidden for too long.

Montenegro would get the students so worked up into a frenzy of excitement that the bus tours turned into debauchery parties. The students did the Tony Robbins thing, hopping around and dancing like lunatics. They dressed up in weird, colorful outfits. You'd have guys running around in pink tutus. I'm not kidding. (A special shout-out to Jordan O. who specifically enjoyed these pink tutus.)

They'd all be screaming, "I'm a millionaire! I'm a millionaire!" It was ridiculous. The bus tours had some good content, but Montenegro put the students into such a frenzied state that they were exhausted by the end. Once they were exhausted, he did his upsell, because he knew their defenses were down and they would be more likely to buy other trainings from him. That's not ethical, and it's not a long-term business plan. Integrity is longevity, and he had none.

Here's the problem with that system. Students would get pumped up, but after they'd leave the training, they'd realize they just paid a ton of money for a three-day dance party. After dropping all that money, they didn't have any support, no one called them back, so they'd get angry. The students would get home and feel duped. They'd think, "What did I just do?"

No matter how many properties Montenegro and Geno sold at their events after I left, more than half of them would unwind. The buyer would demand their money back. Montenegro sold properties with ego and cockiness, not with truth and trust. And his staff was poorly trained. His students soon figured out they weren't in good hands. People are not stupid.

When I was running things, they would buy because they sensed the integrity. When something went wrong, they saw the communication immediately and watched us try to make it right. That was the security they needed in order to let go of their hard-earned money and buy property three thousand miles away to be managed. They did it because they believed in me. Neither one of those idiots realized that until their properties started unwinding.

These two egomaniacs created their own shit sandwich and had to eat it. They had dozens of properties unwinding and customers who were pissed off. They had complaints coming in daily. At some point, Montenegro had enough of it and gave Geno his walking papers. Montenegro didn't even have enough class to fire Geno himself; he had one of his minions call Geno and say, "We're not going to be working with you anymore." Just like that.

So ultimately, Geno got screwed by Montenegro in much the same way I did.

Those two haven't been working together for years. Basically, they found out I wasn't just a fucking broker. I was the backbone and soul of that whole property business. I proposed it, I created it, I brought it in, I kept the wheels on, and I was the glue that kept it running right. That's what they didn't understand. That's why they failed.

THEY FOUND OUT I WASN'T JUST A FUCKING BROKER. I WAS THE BACKBONE AND SOUL OF THAT WHOLE PROPERTY BUSINESS.

UNANSWERED PRAYERS

When I launched my training company in January 2014, we had massive success right out of the gate. We're still going strong today and growing every year.

I went through hell to reach heaven, and I don't regret a minute of it. I'm thankful for everything. I'm in the place I need to be, and I've embraced it. Through the hardship, I discovered my real purpose, and the path became clear to me. The farther I move away from the old toxic atmosphere, the more I understand my destiny is in helping others and treating all people with dignity and respect.

My company, Nick Vertucci Real Estate Academy (NVREA), is thriving. We are known as the best in this business because we keep our promises to students and provide the best training ever. When people come to work here, they know it's a privilege. They know that we have integrity and that we do what we say. They know they will be told the truth and treated with respect.

We've been so successful that we launched the National Real Estate Network (NREN), our second real estate brand. Our reputation is unsoiled, which has never happened in this industry, so we're going to continue to push forward with both the NVREA and NREN brands. And I have no doubt much more is to come.

Over time, we've built a massive network of investors, between our staff, mentors, and students. Every investor in our network has the same goal and the same mission and does business the same way, with the same training. We're thousands of students strong now. All of this has been a major blessing for everyone, especially the students.

As for Montenegro, I think he still goes on stage, but it's no longer the massive stage he once had. Now he mostly moonlights at real estate investment clubs and real estate expos. That's where the has-beens in this industry go to die. In contrast, my business is flourishing. In fact, it's larger than his business was at its peak. And I'm still just getting started.

BETRAYAL BROADENED MY SHOULDERS

This experience was one of the toughest emotional and mental challenges that I ever had to overcome. It was a level of emotional devastation that could have destroyed me if I'd let it. If I hadn't gone back to my training, to pattern interruption, and to a beast-mode mind game, plus the four steps (see it, believe it, map it, execute it), I wouldn't have survived. Don't forget, your mind and your resolve are your strongest assets.

If I hadn't worked relentlessly morning, noon, and night, in addition to having a strong mind game, I wouldn't have made it. Sometimes, when I'm standing in front of hundreds of students at a bus tour, I remember what I've been through, and I wonder how I made it this far. Here's how: I took one step at a time, worked harder than anyone else, and with relentlessness, I came out on top. Sometimes I look out at the massive crowd, and it's surreal and gives me such a rush of accomplishment. Winning in business is a great feeling.

SOMETIMES I LOOK OUT AT THE MASSIVE CROWD, AND IT'S SURREAL AND GIVES ME SUCH A RUSH OF ACCOMPLISHMENT. WINNING IN BUSINESS IS A GREAT FEELING.

I was catapulted into this business by default, and it's the best thing that ever happened to me. When it was happening, I would've told you it was the worst thing that ever happened to me. I was rocked emotionally because even though I'm kind of a hard-ass, I'm extremely sensitive when it comes to relationships. I was gutted. People turned their backs on me, friends of mine, because they were afraid of Montenegro and didn't have the guts to stand by me. I had many good friendships with employees at Montenegro's company, and they shunned me. He scared them so much that they were afraid to have any communication with me. It was devastating at the time.

WHAT IS THE TAKEAWAY FROM THIS?

Who knows if I would've even gotten into this business if he hadn't done what he did to me. Who knows if I would've had the gumption to do it. But I do know it fueled me. Every missile he sent into my bunker made me stronger and hardened my resolve.

In the end, he created his own competition. His ego, insecurity, vindictiveness, and lack of integrity are the tragic flaws that led to his downfall and cost him dearly. He created exactly what he feared—a competitor who was better than he was.

After everything that happened, after all the pain and anguish, I believe it was the biggest positive that ever happened to me. It was also the most gut-wrenching thing I ever experienced. Funny how sometimes those two things go together. The readers need to keep this story in mind when they're going through their own storms in business and in life. Sometimes there's a reason and a purpose for the hardships of life.

SOMETIMES THERE'S A REASON AND A PURPOSE FOR THE HARDSHIPS OF LIFE.

The following chapters contain the many lessons that I learned throughout my struggles. If you follow the principles explained in the remainder of this book, you can achieve your goals and overcome any setback and come out better on the other side. You will absolutely come out stronger. Trust me, I know from personal experience.

CHAPTER SEVEN

—

RISE AND GRIND

As you can see, when I decided to start my real estate training company, I had a long list of challenges working against me. I didn't know the training business. I had to learn it as I was launching my company. Millions of dollars of my money were being withheld from me, so I had to go into debt to start the business. I had mounting legal fees as I fought to get that money. And I had somebody with deep pockets and an evil streak coming after me, trying to put me out of business. He made himself my sworn enemy, and he used every dirty trick in the book to destroy me, professionally and personally.

But I started my training business anyway.

The one thing I had going for me was my determination to succeed and my willingness to grind it out until it succeeded. I saw it, I believed it, I mapped it, and I executed it. My story is a good example of overcoming adversity, pushing through obstacles, and continuing to grind when everyone around me was saying, "Hey, why don't you just go try something else? Is this really worth it, Nick?"

I tell my students this story. It's important for them to understand that they're going to have people challenging them along the way. It might be a rival competitor, it might be a former partner, it might be a divorce, or it might be a relative. Maybe it's the economic hardship of losing a job or trying to raise a child. Maybe it's just the time crunch because you're still working another job until you can get your business going. Everyone has their own dream snatchers and naysayers.

BE A GRINDER

Many self-help books present similar theories on success, and all of them seem to use the right words. But the truth of self-help is that success doesn't happen overnight. I'm not saying somebody couldn't luck into creating a miraculous invention and make millions, but that rarely happens. Also, that isn't easy. There aren't any free lunches that I've ever found.

Anything I've ever accomplished has required a ton of sweat equity, burning the midnight oil, and just not stopping until the goal is achieved. The term for that is "grinding."

In this business, you might make fifty offers on properties and not have one of them accepted. When you do finally have an offer accepted, by the time you're done flipping the property, you might make $50,000 in 120 days. My point is, if you stopped at the forty-ninth offer because you became discouraged, you would never flip that one property. If you stop cold-calling, you might never land that one customer who brings in a lot of money. If you give up or stop grinding, if you're lazy, or if you become distracted, you might miss out on a big deal or, maybe even worse, miss out on your destiny.

You need a written plan—or as I refer to it, a map—that describes exactly what you're going to do, and then you have to start taking action and keep following that map until you succeed. You can't give up. That doesn't mean that if you have a flawed model or something that doesn't work, you can't adjust and improve the plan. In my business, we work by duplication. Thousands of people follow our plan within our nationwide community, so we know it works.

When I teach my students, if I paint a picture that everything's rosy or that everyone's going to become rich right away, I'm only setting my students up for discouragement. They'll give up because I've given them a vision of quick success that might not fit the reality they experience.

What I like to tell people is, "Have a vision of reality."

The reality is that no success comes without some pain, without a lot of grinding, and without having to push through the tough spots where other people don't push through. That's why only a certain number of people are truly successful, and most never reach that level. The biggest difference is consistency and a strong mind game. To put it simply, hard work consistently over time leads to success.

TO PUT IT SIMPLY, HARD WORK CONSISTENTLY OVER TIME LEADS TO SUCCESS.

HUSTLE OR DIE

When I first went into the real estate business and started investing, I didn't have a lot of success. I ran into a lot of roadblocks, but I just kept pushing. I kept calling, meeting with people, and learning the business out in the field. I constantly flew to other states to interview management companies in order to figure out how to buy properties in each market. I worked to build relationships with reps, to make connections and partnerships, one at a time. Then all of a sudden, after a long time and a lot of hard work, a bunch of offers were accepted, and I moved up to the next level.

Getting there required constant hustle, and I mean constant. I had no office, so I sat in a coffee shop with a laptop, a phone, and a plan. No matter what, I made those calls. I didn't quite know what the hell I was doing, but I followed what I was taught and made the calls and contacted people. I continued to do that until I started closing deals.

I recommend sitting down each night before bed and writing out everything you want to accomplish the next day. Put tasks in order of priority. Then update it as you go, crossing off each item as you complete it. Work your way through that list no matter what. This can be done daily, weekly, monthly, yearly, and so on. Set your actions and goals and keep hitting them until you arrive at your destiny.

What matters is what makes money, and the focus in this business is to make offers. If you have offers accepted, lock them in and make sure the numbers are right. Even if you're not in the real estate business, there are a certain number of prioritized actions that need to be done in order to create revenue. Do those things first because everything else becomes a lot easier with revenue. Just don't stop hustling!

JUST DON'T STOP HUSTLING!

EVERYTHING GOES BETTER WITH REVENUE

Without revenue, every task becomes stressful and distracting. Focus on the things that make money and be prepared to do a ton of those activities, especially in the beginning. Write them down on a pad of paper and make sure you do them every day, scratching each one off as you go.

When I first started in the real estate business in 2004, I had no money. I was literally busted and drowning in debt. I found it hard to sit there every single day and take action. I had to remind myself to go one door at a time, one call at a time, one deal at a time. The way to one hundred deals is to pick up the phone and make one call at a time.

I didn't have the finances to pay my bills. I had a wife, two kids, and another one on the way. But I had to just block it all out and go to work, or else I would have continued to sink. Most people allow themselves to sink because they're paralyzed by fear and inaction. They don't think it's possible to pull out of their downward spiral, and they just mentally curl up into a ball. When that happens, the situation gets worse and worse, and they become more negative. I know because I lived through this.

MOST PEOPLE ALLOW THEMSELVES TO SINK BECAUSE THEY'RE PARALYZED BY FEAR AND INACTION.

CREATE NEW PATTERNS OF SUCCESS

I have students who procrastinate. I have students who like to focus just on minutiae and all the small stuff. I have students who are such control freaks that they can't do anything great because they have to do everything themselves. Everyone has their patterns of behavior that are ingrained into them, good and bad. If you want to achieve success, you have to create the right patterns of thought and behavior.

Maybe the pattern ingrained into you says, "Just go punch the clock and work a regular job." That way, you don't have to take any calculated risks or go outside of your comfort zone. If that's your pattern, then you're going to have to intentionally force yourself to take calculated risks. Change your environment, change the people you surround yourself with, and start working against the pattern. If your pattern is procrastination, then make yourself accountable to somebody—a partner or a friend—to force yourself to get stuff done.

If you want different results in life, you have to follow a map that is different from the one you've been following. If your actions create mediocrity, you'll be mediocre. If you want more than that, create a different plan, write it out, and put it into action. Look at what's working for other people and then duplicate it.

You have to create new patterns of success. Learn what other people have been successful doing. Then you can go beyond what they're doing to make it better, improve their plan, and take it to a higher level. That's what I did. I'm not a rocket scientist. I didn't create some magic formula. I took formulas that had been out there for decades and updated them and put my personal touch on them.

Once you have a written map for what you want to accomplish, take the steps to make it happen. If you see yourself falling back into the old pattern of procrastination, saying, "I'll do that tomorrow," or "I'm going to work on that after our son's wedding in August," just put a stop to it. Work your ass off and give your son a better wedding.

GOALS ARE A STEPPING STONE TO YOUR VISION

As part of your plan, set some concrete goals. Maybe you want to create a certain amount of wealth, or maybe you want to close a certain number of deals. You need personal goals that you can shoot for. That helps you keep moving forward. I constantly compete with myself. I say, "Here's where I've gotten myself thus far, so now I need to take it to another level."

What's your next goal? What's the next big prize you're working toward? Is it $5 million in net worth, $10 million, or more? It's not always about money. Maybe your goal is to create more free time, so you need to buy fifteen more cash flow properties in order to do that. Maybe you want to create enough money to fund a specific charity that you care about. Whatever that prize is, you have to know what you're after and what you're working toward.

What is it that you want? Whatever it is, keep focusing on it until you achieve it. Once you do, then create even loftier goals. Goals are stepping stones to your vision.

SUCCESSFUL PEOPLE FAIL OFTEN

Very rarely does someone find huge success the first time they try something. Yes, it has happened a few times, and you might have heard some of those stories. But generally speaking, most entrepreneurs have at least one good, solid failure under their belts, and sometimes many failures. Either they started a business and it wasn't a good idea, or they worked at it for a while, but the market changed, or the industry changed, or the economy changed.

I feared failing because it's an ego crush and it's embarrassing. I have experienced that bitter taste of failure more than once. I think it is more admirable to have tried and failed than to have been too scared to even try. Your other choice is to embrace mediocrity and punch a clock working for someone else. Maybe that's what you want out of life. No harm, no foul. There's nothing wrong with being a hard worker and punching a clock. However, if you're doing that because you're afraid you might fail, then it's tragic. Let me settle the issue right now. Yes, you probably will fail, and that's OK. Just pull up your boot straps and sack up and give it another whack.

I THINK IT IS MORE ADMIRABLE TO HAVE TRIED AND FAILED THAN TO HAVE BEEN TOO SCARED TO EVEN TRY.

People make fun of President Trump because he had multiple businesses that went bankrupt. But at the same time, the man is worth billions of dollars now. Oh, and I said *President* Trump. Love him or hate him, that's not the point here. Don't get distracted by politics. Do you know what he endured to become president? He keeps putting himself out there, and he keeps grinding away. He doesn't care about people judging him for his failures because he knows it's going to happen. Failure builds character, and if you can push through, it won't break you.

FAILURE BUILDS CHARACTER, AND IF YOU CAN PUSH THROUGH, IT WON'T BREAK YOU.

THE ENTREPRENEUR

There is something I wrote a few years ago that I like to read to my students. I call it "The Entrepreneur."

THE ENTREPRENEUR
Nobody knows the time put in.
Nobody knows the sacrifices made.
Nobody knows the rejection.
Nobody knows the criticisms.
Nobody knows about the empty bank accounts.
Nobody knows the fear that had to
be fought and conquered.
Nobody knows the sleepless nights
putting together your vision.
But...
Someday your success will speak for itself.
#GrindItOut.

If you're an entrepreneur, if you're someone who wants to be great, you're going to put in time that nobody realizes. You're going to make sacrifices that the normal person wouldn't make. Nobody knows the rejection because when you're in business, you are rejected a lot. You have a lot of people telling you no. Nobody knows the criticisms because, honestly, people love to criticize success or your lack of success along the way. Nobody knows the empty bank accounts because sometimes success doesn't start off like a bowl of cherries, and it's rough financially for a while. Nobody knows the fear that has to be fought and conquered because if you want to become great, there are many things to fear, such as losing money, losing reputation, and losing your business.

Nobody knows the sleepless nights putting together your vision because it requires a lot of mental energy when you're building something or when you're struggling or when you're trying to plow through a hard time. But some day, your success will speak for itself. What most people see when they look at a successful person is the end of the rainbow. They don't understand what it took to get there.

IS YOUR WHY IMPORTANT ENOUGH?

One tactic that will fuel your activity and keep you grinding forward is to find your why. This is so cliché and used so often. Why do you want success? Why do you want your own business? Everyone has a why. Some might say it's their kids. They want to leave something to their kids, or they want to take care of a spouse or an elderly parent. Whatever your why, is it important enough to you that you'll keep going even when it hurts, even when you're scared?

WHATEVER YOUR WHY, IS IT IMPORTANT ENOUGH TO YOU THAT YOU'LL KEEP GOING EVEN WHEN IT HURTS, EVEN WHEN YOU'RE SCARED?

Is your why important enough to sustain you when things don't go perfectly on your first deal? I can't make it important enough to you, and I can't follow you around in your real estate career, or any business for that matter. I can give you the network, I can give you the community, I can give you the support, but I can't give you the drive. I can't give you the "don't give up" attitude. I can't give you the "keep pushing and grinding" commitment. That's something you're going to have to find within yourself and do it.

When you're disappointed in this business, it's tempting to blame the process. The process isn't the problem. If you give up, you're the problem. Some of the students I went through my real estate training with are no longer in the business. They all had the same instruction that I did. Most of them were probably way more book smart than I am. Then why have I achieved success in real estate while they haven't? Because I decided I was going to succeed no matter what. I saw that success in my mind, I made myself believe it, I put together a plan, I mapped it with the steps I needed to take to get there, and then I executed it by grinding day after day until I reached where I am. See it, believe it, map it, execute it.

I DECIDED I WAS GOING TO SUCCEED NO MATTER WHAT.

No matter what came my way, I pushed it aside and kept going forward and focusing on doing the tasks that would generate revenue. That's what you have to do if you want to succeed, and nobody can make the decision to do it for you. Don't blame others when it doesn't work, because it's working for thousands of people. If it doesn't work for you, it's not the program's fault. It's not your college's fault. It's not your parents' fault. You own it. Be accountable.

QUITTING IS WORSE THAN FAILING

How did I overcome all the hardships I faced when starting my business? From the legal attacks to the money problems, from the steep learning curve to the deep, abiding fear, what was my secret? Honestly, I can't attribute overcoming those hardships to anything other than sheer grit and an absolute will to win by never quitting or giving up.

I CAN'T ATTRIBUTE OVERCOMING THOSE HARDSHIPS TO ANYTHING OTHER THAN SHEER GRIT AND AN ABSOLUTE WILL TO WIN BY NEVER QUITTING OR GIVING UP.

I was conscious of what was in my way, and I just said, "This is not going to beat me. I don't care what I have to do. I don't care if I have to work seven days a week. I don't care if I have to live in a cardboard box. I refuse to let any of these people, any of these situations, or any of what's in front of me win. If anybody can achieve this success, then I know I can do it. It's simply a matter of grinding it out until I make it happen." I willed it into existence.

I had plenty of excuses I could have used to procrastinate.

I could have said, "Now's not the time to start a new business. Let me get my money back first; I don't want to risk more debt in case I never see the money that's owed to me. I don't want to be sued. I know he's going to sue me, and I know when he does, it might cost seven figures. I'd better wait. I'll put this off another year." But I didn't say that to myself.

Instead, I said, "I have every right to be in this business. I know I can do it better, so I'm doing it. I'm going to make it work, despite every circumstance and every challenge."

I had every opportunity to quit, and I had every reason to quit. I had every reason to decide the time wasn't right, but I didn't do that. As I like to say, what's the best time to plant an oak tree? Twenty-five years ago. What's the second-best time? Right the fuck now is. Not tomorrow, not after your son's wedding. Not after someone promises they're going to leave you alone. Now.

NO TRACTION WITHOUT ACTION

Traction is just a product of action. It's a product of grinding and hustling. If you keep doing something long enough, if you keep pounding away, you're going to see results. If you make your first fifty offers on houses and none is accepted, but then you finally have one accepted, that's traction. Then you run the numbers, and it works, and you close on the property and take control of it. That's traction. Apply this to any industry and business. I'll use real estate investing as my example.

Then you find the right contractor and put the money in place to start the deal moving, and that's traction. You have your first deal flipped, and you put the profit in your bank account, and that's some real traction. It builds over time, which creates results, which strengthens your belief system, and your belief system gives you absolute certainty that you will succeed. Absolute certainty allows you to take more action. More action creates more results, which produces momentum. That's how it works.

Picture a big, slow-moving diesel truck. It's just grinding along, belching smoke. Then it picks up a little speed, it starts to gain momentum. Finally, it's just trucking down the road, hauling ass, but it takes time and a lot of energy to reach cruising speed.

The first time I realized I was making it happen is when I closed my first deal. It wasn't even a cash flow property, which was my specialty. I was buying a lot in Utah. I came up with the idea to buy lots up in Traverse Mountain and, with construction loans, to start building properties on actual tracts of land. When I sold the first one of these properties and turned a tidy profit, I looked at the property and thought, "Making that amount of money would have taken a year of my life at one point."

The first deal is always the hardest. It seems so unattainable, but once you finally bring it to completion, it feels so good that it's surreal. I tell my students that your first deal is kind of like your first kiss. You've never done it before, and you're scared to death. You know you want to. You don't even know why you want to, but you know that it's good. Then you do it, and you're like, "I'm going to do that again." You improve and get better each time.

THE INDUSTRY'S BLACK EYE

The real estate training industry has a bad reputation and a huge black eye. They charge a whole lot of money to teach students good theory in training, but they don't always teach them how to execute. They don't teach the reality of what's going to happen and the challenges students will face out there. Instead, they provide cursory theoretical training, and then students learn the real deal out in the field. As a result, many students find themselves in over their heads.

When I first started buying real estate, before I had that one-on-one mentorship with Cris, I made some mistakes. I was involved in buying preconstruction lots, but I didn't know how to prepare the lot for building. I missed a million steps that weren't taught to me, so I had to learn them the hard way. The process took longer because I wasn't prepared.

That's why I give students a strategy, and along with it, I give them a detailed, practical game plan for every moving part. I clarify all the challenges that are going to come with it and all the possible pitfalls, because I want them to be prepared for the reality of it. I don't want them to be caught off guard.

The biggest mistake students make, even if they have the best training, is that they skip certain steps because they think they can do better. My program has been duplicated a million times because it works. That's why franchising exists. People buy Subway franchises because they have a proven success formula. Their system has figured out the right pricing structure, an efficient way to make sandwiches, the right balance of meat and bread, hiring, marketing, and so on. It works, and it turns a profit for franchise owners all over the world. But if someone goes rogue and tries to alter the Subway system, regardless of how many times they've been told not to, if they insist on doing it their own way, it's probably going to cause trouble. I always say color within the lines.

Another mistake students make is to go too fast. Instead of buying one or two properties and getting a feel for it, they try to do too much too soon. Start by putting your money into one property. Don't try to do twenty deals and have twenty offers accepted. Do you want to make mistakes times twenty or times one?

When you make your first deal, you learn, and you work some of the rough edges off. Then you're ready to do two more deals, and if those go well, you're in the groove and ready for three. Pace yourself. Don't try to conquer the whole world on your first time out. You'll wind up over your head and overwhelmed, and when that happens, you'll feel like curling up into a ball and dying. Apply this practice to any business or investment.

DON'T GO ROGUE

Most of the training companies out there will teach you to go rogue and jump into real estate with both feet. They'll say, "Fire your boss! Quit your job. Go all-in."

Don't do it.

Most people who quit their jobs won't have any income coming in, so they're hard-pressed to make deals work. The clock's ticking. Trying to rush deals can lead to bad decisions. You're probably not going to become a millionaire in the first ninety days, and if someone tells you that, they're misleading you.

Students and new investors have stars in their eyes. They want what other people have. They want to go out there and hit the fast track. I can identify with that. I did a lot of stuff pretty fast myself, but it's a mistake. If someone tells you, "Crush it. Go out there and do as many deals as quickly as you can," they're setting you up for disappointment.

Before I got into real estate, I was a police officer for many years. When someone is a brand-new police officer, just out of the academy, you put them with a training officer for the first few months. Why? Because even though they went through the academy, there's a learning curve. Training is important, but it's different when you go out there and try to do the job for real. It feels different. Have a mentor if possible, and figure it out one deal at a time until you have it down.

You don't take a new cop and have them go alone into a bank that's getting robbed. Senior officers take charge of that kind of situation, and the new officers observe and learn. Over time, the new officers are able to do more and more, and they can handle a situation like that. Once you begin doing the job in the real world, over time, it becomes natural. Five years later, you're a cop, and you're doing things in your sleep. The job becomes a reflex.

Remember I said reflex, not routine. Complacency is

what gets cops killed. They let their guard down because of routine. Same for investing in anything. Don't let your guard down, or you can lose your financial life. Reflex is much different. That's what saves cops' lives. Train enough and do something over and over so that in a stress situation when your bodily reflexes shut down, you're on autopilot from your training. Same with your financial lives. They should be protected by constant training of your investing reflexes.

In any business, it's first about safety. Then once you've learned how to do things safely, it's about speed and getting things done faster. Finally, it's about money and maximizing profit.

YOUR CHEESE WILL GET MOVED

I don't care how lucrative your business is or how good your market is, you never know when adversity will strike. All economies turn. Technologies change. Sometimes your business gets taken from you, or people screw you over. You have to know that up front. Expect it and build your lifestyle accordingly.

When I started my computer business, I thought it would never end, but I was naive. I built a level of personal living expense that I couldn't sustain. I didn't have money intelligence. Right now, I drive a nice car, I have a lot of nice things, but I'm always conscious of the bottom line. I don't have any debt. My business might not last forever. The economy could change drastically, or there could be a big regulation overhaul in my industry. You never know. If it all ends tomorrow, what's my game plan? For me, I'm good now. I'll be ready to deal with it. I learned the hard way once but never again.

How does a guy like Mike Tyson wind up broke? He made millions of dollars per fight. He didn't understand that nothing lasts forever. You can always spend more than you make. If things dry up and you have too much debt, you're going to be buried.

Whatever your business is, hit it hard now while you can because it might not last. Where are you at today? Can you live off what you have? Do you have enough? If you don't, you better start grinding harder and a lot smarter.

CAN YOU LIVE OFF WHAT YOU HAVE? DO YOU HAVE ENOUGH? IF YOU DON'T, YOU BETTER START GRINDING HARDER AND A LOT SMARTER.

CHAPTER EIGHT

INTEGRITY

In the real estate training business, and in any business, integrity creates longevity. Yet so many real estate training companies care only about making a fast buck. There's no real passion for the students; it's just about making money off them. These training companies herd people through training, but they maintain no connection with them afterward. Because of that lack of support and follow-up, most of their students fail. Then the company's reputation suffers, and the company ultimately fails. Apply this to any business: Integrity is longevity.

I was taken advantage of big-time when I took my first real estate training. I didn't have the knowledge I needed to protect myself. The whole experience left a sour taste in my mouth, as it did for thousands of others like me. But I took accountability, I didn't blame others, I learned from it, and I became wiser and stronger.

I TOOK ACCOUNTABILITY, I DIDN'T BLAME OTHERS, I LEARNED FROM IT, AND I BECAME WISER AND STRONGER.

I wouldn't be where I am today if I hadn't gone through that process. As I learned about this industry, I began to understand that a lack of integrity was the norm. Most companies don't call customers back. They don't work with them if there are problems. They just don't care about the students once the training is done. It's a "churn 'em and burn 'em" mentality.

These kinds of companies burn themselves out. They earn a bad reputation because of the way they neglect students, so they have to shut down that brand. A few months later, they find some new celebrity to put on the marketing banners and start all over again. Worst of all, the students have no protection. I don't care what business or industry you work in, the takeaway is simple: Provide the best product or service in your industry. Stand behind it better than your competition. And play long ball with your reputation.

PROVIDE THE BEST PRODUCT OR SERVICE IN YOUR INDUSTRY. STAND BEHIND IT BETTER THAN YOUR COMPETITION. AND PLAY LONG BALL WITH YOUR REPUTATION.

AN OPPORTUNITY WASTED

Taco Montenegro had a golden opportunity. He had limited competition. He had his own TV show that he could leverage to attract students to his trainings. Basically, he had everything going for him, but emotionally he led with greed and ego. He didn't care about anyone else. Outwardly, he said all the right things, but deep down, he didn't care at all about the students—or the people who worked for him. He cared only about money and ego.

Because of his lack of integrity, he burned out his brand. He basically lost the business on his own because he didn't follow through and do the right things. He ran the business into the ground.

You must capitalize on opportunity. You must lead by example, not by fear. Never take for granted your blessings, clients, and the people who work for you. Don't be fearful of the greatness of others; recognize it, harness it, and create leaders who will die for your cause with you.

INTEGRITY CREATES LONGEVITY

Always do things with integrity. Always. Not just because of the money, not just to avoid running your business into the ground, but because it's the right thing to do.

In my training business, we do exactly what we say we're

going to do. Our philosophy is that the student is always right, even if they aren't. If we say we'll provide a service and communicate with students, we do it. If any link in the chain breaks and a member of my team drops the ball, I'm on it immediately because without integrity, without your reputation and name, you're nothing. That's something I always tell my students.

We have a private Facebook page for investors that has thousands and thousands of members. In that community, we take our students to a higher level of training and keep them engaged long after the classes are over. I tell the investors, "It's a privilege to be in this network. It's not an entitlement, so if you start making deals with other students in this network and you lack integrity or if you take advantage of people or if you don't follow through on your promises, you're out." I have kicked many people out who weren't doing business the right way. It doesn't matter if they're paying students. We do business with integrity, and that's it. I share that promise from the stage, and I stick to it.

Even when I was heavily involved in cash flow investing, before I started my training company, I worked with other investors who were buying my properties, and I didn't receive one complaint. In thousands of properties and deals, I never had a single complaint because I always worked from a place of service rather than ego. I was never just selling something. I always tried to make things right, even when it was painful. I made things right because my reputation was on the line.

I could raise millions of dollars of capital with private lenders and other people I've worked with just because of my reputation. Why? Because I've always kept my word, I've always made things right, and people know it. You never have to worry about me in business.

When you work with integrity, it pays off because word gets around. People hear through the grapevine whether you are honest or whether you cannot be trusted. Your reputation precedes you, and that's why I say integrity creates longevity. If you don't do business the right way, opportunities will dry up.

IF YOU DON'T DO BUSINESS THE RIGHT WAY, OPPORTUNITIES WILL DRY UP.

DON'T BATTLE OVER SMALL AMOUNTS OF MONEY

Just because I stood against my former partners on principle does not mean you stand on principle in every little thing. What you're looking for with your customers and when you're in business with people is a long-term relationship. Usually, it's not worth fighting over something small if you're playing long ball.

I used to have to fight with my former partners on a regular basis about how our reputation is bigger than any one small dispute, even when the client was clearly wrong. If we hang our hat on that and refuse to budge, we may get some bad press. Then we have to deal with that going forward, possibly for years. Other people might read that bad press and, as a result, miss out on the great things we offer. I always had to paint the bigger picture for them. Think long term; don't squabble over small disputes just on principle.

There are times when you could stand on principle and say to a client, "Look, here's what the contract says, and here's what you did." Maybe the client is in the wrong about something, and you can prove it. You don't want to absorb the financial loss, or you don't want to give something back, or you don't want to give in when you know the client is wrong.

In those situations, you can pull out the contract, take a hard line, and win the small battle. But by doing so, you color that client's perception of your organization. They might come back to haunt you. They might go tell fifteen other people a story about you that isn't true just to get back at you.

My point is, don't be shortsighted when it comes to disagreements and problems with a client. In every business, there are occasional misunderstandings with customers or times when a client genuinely feels wronged in some way. Learn to play long ball in those situations. That's when you need to think long term.

However, by no means should you let people deliberately or dishonestly take advantage of you or your business. That's a dangerous precedent to set. If someone is trying to cheat you or scam you out of money, that's probably a time to dig your heels in and fight.

LONG-TERM VERSUS SHORT-TERM MENTALITY

You have bigger and better things to do than to try and make a quick buck. You're trying to create long-term wealth, and you don't do that with a short-term mentality. Look at your business as a long-ball game.

> **YOU'RE TRYING TO CREATE LONG-TERM WEALTH, AND YOU DON'T DO THAT WITH A SHORT-TERM MENTALITY. LOOK AT YOUR BUSINESS AS A LONG-BALL GAME.**

Your goal should not be purely to make the maximum amount of money out of a deal. Your goal should be to view every deal as a stepping stone toward your larger vision, and your vision is bigger than any one deal. Your bigger vision is what you build, what you want to accomplish. It's your name, your integrity, your financial life, and your retirement.

If there's a dispute and you're in the right, you could stick to your guns, but think carefully about what that will do for you long term. Look, I don't roll over easily. If someone attacks me, if I am sued in court, I fight back. I'm relentless. But when it comes to little things such as a small business deal, I generally concede because it's not worth leaving a stain on the big picture of what I'm trying to achieve.

The same goes for taking advantage of people. Even if you can get away with it, it's never worth it. It's not the right thing to do, and the universe has a way of coming back around and getting revenge. Don't do it.

PLAY TO YOUR STRENGTHS, HIRE YOUR WEAKNESSES

Always play to your strengths. I'm the leader of my company; I have hundreds of people who work for me, with me, and around me. My name is on the brand, my face is on the banner, and I call the shots. There's no question about that. I don't have any other owners. However, I never try to be something I'm not. I never pretend like I'm the smartest guy in the room.

My former partner did that often. At all costs, even if he knew he wasn't, he tried to pretend he knew more than everyone else about everything. He always presented himself as the expert about everything. People knew it wasn't true. Sooner or later, oil rises to the top of the water, and you can't hide the fact that you have certain weaknesses.

If you're a good leader, if you're smart in business, you play to your strengths. You stay in your lane. You do what you're good at. I have people working around me who are better in their respective areas than I am, and we all know it. What I'm good at is big-vision stuff. I'm good at communicating, and I'm good at putting deals together. My deal-making instincts are solid, and I have broad shoulders to carry calculated risks. I'm the one who will take calculated risks and make decisions. And I am good at winning in business. That's what I'm good at.

I have people in my company who are better than I am when it comes to other skills, such as construction or accounting. I build leaders. I build people who want to be part of something bigger, and I don't try to out-ego them, step on them, or keep them down. My former partner did that. If he felt threatened at all by another person's talent or ability, he crushed them, fired them, or turned them in a different direction. If you're a great leader, you can't be threatened by other talent. The more talents you have around you, the better your company is going to be and the better you're going to be.

I'm nothing without the people around me. They're nothing without me because I created this company and this movement. Never downplay your value and who you are or let anyone do that to you. But at the same time, you have to develop leaders. Build up people who have passion about your movement, your vision, and your company. If you do that, their strengths become your strengths.

If you're in this business and you're making a ton of money from your strategy, stay in your lane as long as you can. Like a running back in football, hit that hole and keep hitting it, and don't try to do something you don't understand or that you're not as good at. Understand your own strengths, then find people who have different strengths than you and build your team accordingly. Play to your strengths; hire your weaknesses.

IF YOU'RE IN THIS BUSINESS AND YOU'RE MAKING A TON OF MONEY FROM YOUR STRATEGY, STAY IN YOUR LANE AS LONG AS YOU CAN.

DON'T BE SELF-CENTERED

Some people do business deals or a joint venture together, and they look at only their side of it. If two people are in a deal, typically, one's providing the money and the other is providing the time and effort, but they are both equally important. The problem is, sometimes neither person is wise enough to see the value the other is bringing to the table. Without the money, you don't have the deal, and without someone putting in the time and the sweat equity, the money doesn't do anything but sit there. This applies to all kinds of business deals and relationships.

Too often, however, the partners wind up resenting each other. The partner putting in all the time and effort begrudges the partner who provided the capital but did no work. The partner providing the money feels like they are shouldering all the risk. Because they are putting up the capital, they feel like they should benefit more, so they undervalue the partner doing the work. That's why sometimes partners do deals and later decide they want to renegotiate.

I always recommend that people try to put themselves in the other person's shoes and see things from their point of view. Don't use self-justification as your guide. If you're only ever trying to justify yourself and your needs, you wind up overvaluing yourself.

I've had talented people in my company who did this. They brought good value, but then they started to overvalue themselves so much that it became impossible to work with them. They're never paid what they think they're worth. They don't put enough value on the people they're working with, so everyone grows tired of trying to work with them.

If you act like that, people will stop working with you. They'll be afraid to begin any kind of business relationship with you because they know your attitude is always going to be "Me, me, me." You'll find yourself constantly looking for new people to partner with, new people to borrow money from, or new people to be the boots on the ground for you. This can be detrimental to your business. Again, this applies to any and all businesses and business deals.

DON'T DEVALUE YOUR TALENT

My former partner overvalued his worth, and he devalued everyone around him, including the people who were key to his success. I'm one of them. I provided him with millions of dollars in revenue, his students loved me, and my three-day training was amazing. I was a huge asset to his company, but when I started being liked by his students or having too much success, he felt threatened. He didn't want me to make the kind of revenue I was making, so he took it away.

But when he took it away, he overvalued himself. He thought he could do the speaking for the three-day classes himself. He thought he could put somebody else in my place on the ground. He thought his company could take care of the customer service and anchor the sales. He was wrong. He overvalued himself and undervalued everyone around him, and without good people around him, he failed. In business, if it ain't broke, don't fix it. Generally, this is a huge mistake. Don't make it in your business.

IT'S NOT ALL ABOUT YOU

People tend to justify their own actions. They focus on their side of events and overstate their own value. If you do that, you'll be blind to how much you need other people in your business. You won't see their value, their input, or their contribution. You'll blow up deals, you'll blow the professional relationship, and you'll blow up future opportunity.

Overvaluing yourself means you'll miss out on future seven-figure decisions. That's why you have to put yourself in the other person's shoes, try to see their value, their side of the situation, and how they want to be treated. How much would you want to be paid if you were in their shoes? What percentage would you think you were worth? Stop being self-centered.

Sometimes when you put yourself in someone else's shoes, it opens your eyes. You realize, "You know, I'm out of line here, and I need to appreciate that relationship. I need to appreciate that capital. I need to appreciate that person's effort on the ground. I need to value their contributions because without them, this part of the business doesn't work." Appreciate people and value them, both personally and monetarily.

Too often, when leaders make outrageous demands, they justify themselves internally, externally, and verbally. They make all kinds of excuses and come up with all sorts of ways to explain their unreasonable demands. You can rationalize anything if you work hard enough at it. But at the end of the day, they're just overvaluing themselves and devaluing the people they work with.

THE NV REAL ESTATE ACADEMY AND THE NATIONAL REAL ESTATE NETWORK

The NV Real Estate Academy (NVREA) has been going strong for years now with an untarnished reputation. I recently launched my second real estate training brand, the National Real Estate Network (NREN), and I'm running it completely hands-on. I do all the teaching myself and make all the decisions. I interact with the customers, and I take care of them every step of the way. I tell my students, "I'm going to give you reality, not reality TV." Maybe because of my experience running the computer business, I always come from a place of customer service and adding value.

Over four and a half years with my previous partner, I saw how not to run a training business. That's why I built my model in the opposite way of most training companies. I focus on providing fulfillment and an active national network of real estate investors. I want to make sure my students are supported by a great network so they can execute after they leave training. I want them to have more than just good theory. I want them to have the type of real estate training that is not just theory but also promotes actual execution and fosters massive financial success.

I WANT THEM TO HAVE THE TYPE OF REAL ESTATE TRAINING THAT IS NOT JUST THEORY BUT ALSO PROMOTES ACTUAL EXECUTION AND FOSTERS MASSIVE FINANCIAL SUCCESS.

Today, I don't focus on selling properties to my students, only on providing great training. The reason I don't sell properties is because my hands are so full running the training business properly that I can't control the properties. Unless I am personally buying and running the properties, personally handling customer service, and personally controlling the whole process from start to finish, I won't touch it. If I have to let someone else run it, I can't guarantee the quality of the properties, and that can put my students at risk. I just won't do that to my students. And I'll never put my own personal reputation in the hands of someone else or their actions.

If I went up on stage and said, "Buy these properties," students would buy them. I know how to sell properties. I know that part of the business more than any other part, but I don't do it. I know what it feels like to be taken advantage of. Unless I control every aspect of a property deal, I can't protect my students, so I don't do it.

I forsake a lot of different revenue streams in this business because of my commitment to integrity. I won't raise a dime from the students for my personal investing. If I wanted to, I could raise millions of dollars from them; that's what other training operators do. They make deals with students and take their money. My employees will be fired immediately if they do a deal with a student because students have stars in their eyes with our staff. They think the staff member or mentor or even myself knows so much, and because we're on stage, they let their guard down. People are taken advantage of that way. I refuse to teach them bad habits.

NVREA and NREN are both going strong and have a massive network of real estate investors who are all highly trained and who network together.

THE INTEGRITY OIL ALWAYS RISES TO THE TOP

Relationships are built over time, and not just from your marketing message. Everybody is going to tell you they're the greatest. Everyone is going to tell you they have the best training company, that they're the best real estate agent, that they're the best whatever. Nobody comes in and says, "I'm going to hustle you, and I have no integrity."

Nobody admits that. They always tell you what you want to hear, but the proof is in the results. Over time, the oil will always rise to the top, and you will know whom you're working with.

NOBODY COMES IN AND SAYS, "I'M GOING TO HUSTLE YOU, AND I HAVE NO INTEGRITY."

The real relationship is built when you have issues, when things don't go perfectly. That's when clients find out if you're for real, when they see you're not walking away from a problem. I've kicked students out of my network simply because they stopped communicating with other students in deals that had challenges. They didn't want to face up to the problem, so I kicked them out. Run your business from a place of service and integrity with your employees and customers. It's a winning strategy.

RUN YOUR BUSINESS FROM A PLACE OF SERVICE AND INTEGRITY WITH YOUR EMPLOYEES AND CUSTOMERS. IT'S A WINNING STRATEGY.

INTEGRITY ATTRACTS QUALITY PEOPLE

You see the real integrity of a person when the chips are down. When everything is going well, you don't see a person's true character. If you stick with people through the problems and the hard times, that's when you build long-term relationships. That's when you really build the equity of your brand and your business. That's when you create more capital and more opportunities, and more people want to work with you, and your business will grow.

Most people in my company have been in this industry for a long time, and they choose to stay with me, no matter what salary they're offered somewhere else. They see that what we're doing is what everyone else always promised they would do but didn't follow through on it. They like being part of something good, something truly valuable. They want to be able to tell students something and see it happen on the back end. When you have employees, it's important to get them to see the business as their own. Then they will want to protect it and treat it as if it's their own.

WHEN YOU HAVE EMPLOYEES, IT'S IMPORTANT TO GET THEM TO SEE THE BUSINESS AS THEIR OWN. THEN THEY WILL WANT TO PROTECT IT AND TREAT IT AS IF IT'S THEIR OWN.

And that's how I treat the people who work for me as well. If I say I'm going to do something, I do it. If I make a promise, I keep it. If a situation won't work out, I'm honest with them. People respect that. I pay them on time, I don't short anyone on their commissions, I don't devalue them, and I don't yell at meetings or belittle people. I create leaders, and I create people who want to be part of something.

That's the way to build a business with integrity.

CHAPTER NINE

PASSION

Find your passion. It's so cliché to say that. We've all heard it a hundred times. Sure, it's great to find what you're passionate about, but that could take years. In the meantime, you have to pay the bills and earn a living. The fact is, most of us will have to spend years working in jobs or businesses we're not passionate about until we find what truly inspires us. It's just part of life.

Back when I started my technology business in 1989, it was a blessing for me in a lot of ways, but technology is so far from what my passion is. Even though I worked hard at it every day, I was really doing it for the money. It was not my passion.

Then I found real estate investing, which I fell in love with. I enjoyed it way more than the computer business. It served as the vehicle for my success. I pursued real estate as hard as I could, and it blessed me with financial success. I love real estate investing, and I always will.

But it wasn't until I launched my real estate training business in January 2014—when I was forty-seven years old—that I feel like I finally built something I could call my passion. It took that long for me to finally start doing something I am truly passionate about, but it was worth the wait. Teaching people how to succeed and win in real estate and in life is what makes me wake up excited and energized every morning.

You might be working in a job that isn't your passion, but you can't afford to leave. That's OK. So are 99.9 percent of people. You have to continue doing what you're doing. You have to pay your bills, so you can't just go pursue your passion. Life doesn't work that way, and sometimes your passion just doesn't translate into dollars—at least not right away. But if you work hard at your passion in your free time, amazing things might just start to happen.

I'LL WORK EIGHTY HOURS TO NOT WORK FORTY

One thing that has always been important to me is my time. Like I say, if you control your time, you control your destiny. I wanted to control my time and my destiny— where I go, what I do, when I wake up, how I wake up. I always say, "I'll work eighty hours a week to not work forty hours a week." Real estate allowed me to create that kind of financial freedom. The bad situation I went through with my former partners pushed me into figuring out my passion, and now I'm doing that.

You can find your passion, even if you have to use a different vehicle to earn your fortune, whether that's real estate investing or some other vehicle. You might have to pursue your passion part time for a while, and that's fine. If you love painting, you might not be able to make a living at it for a long time, so you have to pay the bills. If you must, work your balls off somewhere else so you can do the things you love, and one day, maybe that side passion of yours will turn into something.

Don't take your eyes off the ball. Don't stop working or taking care of your family, but pursue your passion. Sometimes that turns into dollars because you become so good at it because you love it.

Some people are alive on the outside, but they're dead inside. They just fall into the daily routine of punching a clock; they disappear into the system. It's unfortunate because you see a lot of people just kind of walking around, driving on the freeway, and going through the motions of life. Many of them are emotionally dead. You only live once, and whatever you do, you have to pursue what makes you happy.

I want to feel alive at all times.

As I mentioned earlier in the book, I worked for years as a police officer, and I loved law enforcement. But I knew in my entrepreneurial spirit that law enforcement was only going to take me to a certain place financially. Everything isn't about dollars, but if you want your freedom, if you want to wake up organically, then you need the financial independence to do that. I knew I had to make a major life decision if I wanted greater financial success.

MY PART-TIME PASSION

Ever since I was a kid, I wanted to be a cop. I thought it sounded like the coolest job. As I built my computer business and hired employees that I could delegate to, it gave me a handle on my time, so I put myself through a night police academy. It took a year, instead of six months, to earn all of my credentials because I had to go slower.

Then I did police work part time at a reserve level. It was the best thing that ever happened to me because I pursued one of my passions, but I did it at a level that was realistic for me. I didn't take my eye off the ball at my business, which helped me reach a different level in life financially. That opened up a lot of other opportunities for me.

You're here to live your life, not somebody else's life. Even if you have to pursue it part time. Or maybe you just have to work harder in order to create more space or revenue. You can hold down a demanding job and still pursue the things that you love.

On a side note, if you are part of law enforcement, emergency services, a fire department, or in our military, I want to personally thank you for your service, but most of all for your sacrifice. You have my full respect.

THE REALITY OF PURSUING YOUR PASSION

I don't want this to be another generic self-help book that promotes success principles without providing the reality behind them. "Take action and find your passion" doesn't mean much if there's no meat behind it. It's not as simple as just doing something you're passionate about. I've seen so many books like that, and they really don't help. Don't take that the wrong way. Being positive and utilizing all the self-help principles is great, and they will make you a happier and better person. But they won't make you rich. You need a solid viable vehicle and a plan to go with it.

When I say find your passion, I'm not just using that phrase. Sometimes you have to keep working hard, however long it takes, at whatever level you can before you can spend all your time on your passion. That's the truth. I see so many people who put on their tie, drive an hour in traffic, work all day, come home, watch TV, fall asleep, and they look dead to me. They feel dead inside, whether they know it or not. Why? For what? It's not worth it. Well, at least for me it's not.

As I mentioned in chapter 4, I don't want to just throw out concepts such as "pursue your passion" that the self-help world loves without attaching a vehicle to them. I want to attach reality to it. Otherwise, you'll read this book and say, "You're telling me to find my passion, but I have to go to work tomorrow. If I don't, I will lose my house. What do you want me to do—sit on the beach and paint because that's what I love? How long is that going to last?"

The reality is that you must find a vehicle that will help you succeed financially while you pursue your passion in your spare time. Real estate investing is a wonderful vehicle for that. You can invest four hours a week, or forty hours a week, to supplement your income and provide the financial cover you need to pursue what you love. And who knows? You might just fall in love with real estate investing like I did.

YOU MIGHT JUST FALL IN LOVE WITH REAL ESTATE INVESTING LIKE I DID.

The world and our economy are set up to put us into a system, almost like we're on a racetrack going around and around. You have to be conscious of the daily routine of the rat race and not get distracted by it. Yes, you have to play the game a little bit in order to survive, but be conscious of it and fight until you reach a better place, the place you want to be. Real estate investing can help you get there, as can many other businesses and ideas.

I had an eighteen-year run in law enforcement, and I wouldn't trade it for anything, even though there was no economic advantage to that line of work for me when I did it. It was part of my identity, but I was putting my life on the line and not making any real money. Why would I do that? Because I loved it.

Somehow, the idea of being in law enforcement always intrigued me, even as a young kid. Maybe it was my personality, I don't know, but I pursued it and did it successfully. I don't regret a minute of it, despite the lack of pay and benefits. In the end, pursue what you love at whatever level you can pursue it. Otherwise, you're not really living.

HOW DO YOU KNOW WHAT YOUR PASSION IS?

The question is, how can you discover what your true passion is? For me, it happened by chance. I figured it out through circumstances. To start you moving in the right direction, however, identify the things you think about a lot of the time. What do you think about when you go to bed and when you wake up? What do you wish you were doing?

The stuff that you wake up thinking about, the stuff that you go to bed thinking about, the stuff that you wish you were doing, that's your passion. When you wake up every morning and you're excited about what you're doing that day, you've found it. When you can go to bed on Sunday night without dreading Monday morning, when you want the weekend to be over so you can go back to work, then you've found it. Never stop trying to figure out what that is, because your passion will change as you go through life.

THE BROADER VALUE

Often, your passion is not so much your profession but the broader value behind it. I'm in the real estate training industry, and as we've discussed, that industry has a stigma attached to it. But that's what I'm in. Despite the stigma, I'm a product of this industry as a student of it myself. After everything I went through, I was broken financially and emotionally, yet somehow, this industry, in spite of all the negatives, became a huge blessing to me.

That doesn't mean I didn't work hard for it. It doesn't mean the industry itself was dying to do anything for me, but it gave me a vehicle to go out there and grind it out until I changed my life financially. It eventually put me in a position to start my own training company and discover my real passion. The broader value behind it is that I now get to do the same thing for thousands of students that the industry did for me. I can help them create the vehicle to achieve their own success.

Some people have found their passion. Some people are teaching children because their passion is to educate. Some people are social workers because they want to help people. In other words, people choose careers that are not necessarily the highest paid professions—especially teachers who are grossly underpaid—because they are pursuing their passion. I say they should continue to do that. Never stop doing what you love.

Are you already pursuing your passion? Great. Real estate investing can be your side hustle, providing the means to do all the things that you want to do financially while continuing to pursue your passion.

If you have found your passion and you are doing it every day, God bless you. Don't stop doing that, because you wake up every day excited. On the other hand, you can keep doing that job you're so passionate about and use real estate investing as a side vehicle to give you all the other things you want in life. The car that you really want to drive, the nice house that you dream about, the luxury vacations that you want but you'll never be able to afford as a teacher, you can have all of those things without quitting the teaching job that you love so much. Real estate investing is a lucrative business if you know what you're doing and if you do it properly.

I tell my students to use real estate as a vehicle to reach the place they want to be financially. Then they can do other things that they dream about, such as starting their own dance studio or tutoring or whatever it happens to be. It opens up opportunities in things that you're passionate about because when you're healthy financially, that's when you can help people. You can't give anyone a hand when you're a broke, starving artist.

I run my training company in the black. I won't run anything in the red just because it's my passion or I feel the need to sacrifice. If I did that, I wouldn't be able to help my students because I'd be broke. But it's not the money that matters to me; it's not the real estate. I'm in this business to help other people because I love it. I love seeing my students succeed and build wealth to win in business and in life.

I LOVE SEEING MY STUDENTS SUCCEED AND BUILD WEALTH TO WIN IN BUSINESS AND IN LIFE.

Even before I launched my own training company, I knew

I loved teaching. I enjoyed seeing students buy their first properties and be so excited about it. I loved seeing the look in their eyes, the realization that this system could take them to another level in their lives. I experienced those same emotions myself when I first started, so I know the look. I love seeing people succeed.

CREATE FINANCIAL SPACE TO PURSUE YOUR PASSION

Even if you're working a job you don't love and it's creating a good income for you, work harder and sell more. Create as much financial space as you can, or as much revenue as you can, so you can find the time and resources to do what you love. Follow your passions in your spare time, and then if those passions turn into dollars someday, you can switch and do that for a living. Until then, stick to what you're doing, because if you quit to pursue your passion and it doesn't create any revenue, you're going to wind up in debt. Be smart about it.

When I began investing in real estate, I had a rough start. But I knew I was onto something, so I hung in there. I just needed more training. Instead of giving up, instead of whining, I thought, "OK, the situation isn't perfect, and right now it's painful, but I'm going to pick myself up, dust my boots off, and keep on grinding."

I was determined to figure it out and make it work. I knew

I just needed the right vehicle. So I went and figured it out. I took my lumps, made my mistakes, fell behind, but then I pressed on. I could visualize myself succeeding in real estate. I could see it. That's the topic of the next chapter.

CHAPTER TEN

SEE IT

As I tell my students, there's a four-step process to anything you want to accomplish in life, any business venture, or any idea. I call the process See It, Believe It, Map It, Execute It. In this chapter, we'll cover the first step.

First, you have to be able to see what your vision is. You have to know exactly what you're going after and what you're trying to do. You are the author of that entrepreneurial idea, whatever it is, so you have to be able to see it clearly and in detail.

Whatever it is you're trying to build, whatever it is you're trying to create or accomplish, you have to visualize it. You have to really see yourself doing it and living it. It can't be anyone else's vision. It has to be your vision so you know what you're moving toward. Make it detailed and personal to you.

DAYDREAM WITH PURPOSE

One of the ways I do that, if I want to create something, is to envision it. In other words, I actually walk it out in my head, and I think about exactly how I want it to look. I envision it as being already done. I know that sounds cliché, but it's what I've done, and it works. I look at what I'm trying to build or what I'm trying to accomplish, and I try to really see it in my mind.

I'm a big daydreamer. I don't mean I just drift off into space and stare at the wall; I daydream with purpose. In the morning, for instance, I'll wake up and daydream about what I want to accomplish that day. I try not to do this at night before bed because then my mind gets going, and I don't sleep. I shelve items at bedtime and deal with them mentally in the morning. Save the beast-mode stuff for the morning and the daytime, or you may not sleep.

SAVE THE BEAST-MODE STUFF FOR THE MORNING AND THE DAYTIME, OR YOU MAY NOT SLEEP.

Sometimes I do this on a macrolevel, and sometimes I do it on a microlevel. The macrolevel includes envisioning big ideas, such as this book. The microlevel refers to daily tasks. This daydreaming is important because you have to create clear steps to follow that will lead you to what you want. Things don't just appear because you have a vague desire. You have to think specifically about what you want to do.

My training company didn't just appear. I had to think about precisely what I wanted to build, what it would look like, sound like, and feel like to have it up and running. What would I see and feel when I was up on stage. I had to see clearly what I wanted to create, the big picture, and how I wanted to run the training sessions. Then I'd work out the steps to make it happen.

DON'T LET THE PAST DICTATE THE FUTURE

Many people have past failures that can become a hindrance when embarking on some new venture or taking a calculated risk. I try not to let what happened in the past hinder me in the present. I try to envision something better.

I've had my share of personal failures, as I've discussed. I lost everything when my technology business tanked. When you have a past like that, it's easy to harbor negative thoughts such as, "This will never work. I'll just fail again," when trying to start something new.

I never let thoughts of failure creep into my mind, even though I knew it was a real possibility. A large percentage of the training companies that try to launch don't make it because this industry is front-heavy, both in terms of the financial investment and the product. The product has to be right at the launch, and you have to nail it right out of the gate. Plus, you're putting a lot of money up front for marketing. If the business doesn't go well, many of these companies can't afford to keep spending, so they fold. They either don't have the guts or the ability to put more on the line until the business succeeds.

I had people tell me that my company wouldn't work because I'd never had a real estate TV show and didn't have any fame to build on. They basically told me I was pissing in the wind. Other people who tried to start similar businesses, who threw their hat into the ring and failed, told me, "Don't do it." But I convinced myself I could make it work. I envisioned it, I saw clearly in my mind how it would work, and I saw the steps it would take to put it together.

Most of my students come to my training with their own bad past experiences. Often, they tell me, "You know, I watched your infomercial, and something in my gut said you were different. I don't know what it was, but I came into this thing skeptical. I'm hoping it will be good, but I'm planning on being disappointed." I have many students who come into the program with that attitude.

Many of them have lost a lot of money. They've been

taken advantage of, and they've had friends and family try to talk them out of coming. Sometimes the friends and family are sincerely trying to help because they're afraid it's a mistake for them to attend the training. I've had many students at the end of the program tell me, "Thank God I didn't let their discouragement stop me."

A significant percentage of the students who show up at the events don't make it all the way through the training. Sometimes just before the bus tour, they drop off because they let fear influence them. It takes real determination to push through. It's not an easy journey, but if they make it through the four-day bus tour, they're always happy they did it. At that point, they understand what they've overcome.

CREATIVE VISION

As I mentioned, I like to do my daydreaming in the morning. That's when I envision my plans and work out the steps in my head. I do some of this during the day as well, particularly if I'm driving. I'll turn off the radio and just think through my plans. Sometimes I'll take voice notes, but most of the time, it's all in my head.

It sounds corny, but what I try to envision most is getting into the end zone, crossing the finish line. I would see myself standing on that stage in front of hundreds of students, teaching them this business, long before I even had the name of the company. I would say to myself over and over, "Why not me? Why not me? Someone else has done it. Why can't I do it? Bullshit, I'm the best in the business. I just have to have the balls to do it. I need a plan, but then I just have to do it."

I have a patio that I've built for myself at my office. I like to sit out there and have a cigar. It looks like I'm doing nothing, screwing off, but I'm actually thinking deeply. Sometimes I will take a notepad, and I'll write down my thoughts, make a few bullet points. I put those notes in my phone, and then I'll refresh myself if there are certain steps I need to take to reach the next one. I make sure to check off every step as I complete it.

LEADERSHIP

In my company now, people follow me. They believe in the vision, my vision, because they see the value we bring to the students. I always say from the stage, "I'm nothing without the amazing people whom I work with." As a leader, you must acknowledge the importance of the people who work with you. If you don't, then you'll have to surround yourself with minions, yes-men, and people who lack the quality to make your business thrive.

A secure leader understands these principles. An insecure

leader needs people they can dominate. I've experienced both types of leadership, so I know the second type doesn't work.

Treat people with respect, give them the freedom to create and lead their area as if it's their own business, and they will be willing to bleed for you. But if you lead as a dictator, you're going to get shanked. The dictatorship always gets toppled. It's inevitable.

> **IF YOU LEAD AS A DICTATOR, YOU'RE GOING TO GET SHANKED. THE DICTATORSHIP ALWAYS GETS TOPPLED. IT'S INEVITABLE.**

Offer a product your workers can feel proud to stand behind. Offer respect, pay people well, and talk straight with them. That's all it takes. People are excited to work in a company with a leader who treats them well and has vision. Make it their vision as well.

TAKE THE NEXT STEP

If you have a goal that you can clearly see, you still won't accomplish it until you develop a firm belief in your vision. Until then, it's only a really cool idea in your head.

If I didn't truly believe I could and would make my dreams happen, my vision would have remained a fairy tale.

It would never have become real. Later, I would have thought about all of the cool things I could have done if my dream came true.

My vision became a lot closer to reality when I took the next step, Believe It. Until then, it was nothing more than something fun to think about.

CHAPTER ELEVEN

—

BELIEVE IT

Once you envision what you want to create, you have to find a way to really believe in it. You must dream about it, think about it, talk a big game, but deep down in your gut, you have to find a way to really believe it. Sometimes we just don't believe the message, even if we're saying it out loud, trying to pump ourselves up. Deep down, many people don't have the confidence to believe in their own ability.

Whether through the power of having mentors, personal affirmations, or pattern interruption, you have to find a way to believe with absolute certainty that you're going to accomplish your goal. Otherwise, chances are it's not going to happen. You're either going to justify not taking the steps, or you'll talk yourself out of it, or someone else is going to talk you out of it. Remember, there are a lot of dream snatchers out there, people who don't want you to attain your goals.

REMEMBER, THERE ARE A LOT OF DREAM SNATCHERS OUT THERE, PEOPLE WHO DON'T WANT YOU TO ATTAIN YOUR GOALS.

Misery loves company, so you're going to have many elements, both internal and external, working to prevent your success. Many people will tell you that you can't do this. They will say that you don't have the ability or that you're not meant for that sort of thing. They'll say things like, "I don't want you to get your hopes up and then be disappointed."

MIND POWER IS ROCKET FUEL

When I went through losing my technology business and I finally sat with my mentor, he taught me to pattern interrupt and taught me the strength of my mind and basically shamed me for my negative attitude. That's the real reason for my success. I was able to push through the mistakes, push through the obstacles, push through the fear. I was taught how to do that and take fear head-on.

When I was rocked again by my partners who circumvented me, even though I had money at that time, I still went through an intense emotional struggle. What helped me through it wasn't my knowledge of real estate. It wasn't because I knew how to start a real estate training company. Ultimately, what got me through it was my ability to carry the load. In my mind, I had the ability to carry the load; I was able to put the pain in its proper place and use it as fuel rather than a deterrent to success. I made it rocket fuel for success.

I MADE IT ROCKET FUEL FOR SUCCESS.

THE FOUR-MINUTE MILE

A great example of how the human mind can either limit us or set us free is the late Roger Bannister, a runner from the 1950s. At that time in history, no one had ever run a four-minute mile. But Bannister understood the relationship between the human mind and self-imposed limitations. He also had a runner's body, of course, and he had the training and the natural ability. Running a four-minute mile was conceivable for him. That's why I tell students to be realistic and pursue something they can conceivably do.

In order to beat the four-minute mile, Bannister had to train hard physically so he could run at that level; but equally important, he had to train his mind. He understood the power of the mind, so he envisioned running the four-minute mile, seeing it, feeling what it would feel like, and believing it was possible as he trained. He practiced visualizing and feeling himself pushing through the burn and the fatigue. He trained his mind to expect it and overcome it.

He ran the first four-minute mile.

What's most interesting is that after Roger Bannister ran a four-minute mile, over the course of the next several years, dozens of runners also ran a four-minute mile. What changed? Did some powerful new supplement come out? No. It happened because after Bannister ran a four-minute mile, everyone believed it was possible. Before, it seemed unattainable, but after Bannister, they knew it was possible. "If Roger can do it, I can do it." That's the power of the mind.

Either you let yourself be restricted by perceived limitations, or you see yourself overcoming those limitations and accomplishing more. You have to believe you can create the type of success you envision because you've conditioned yourself to see it and believe it.

ACTION CREATES BELIEF

I tell students, if your belief level is low, the only way you're going to raise it is by taking action. If your goal is to run a marathon, but you don't believe you can do it, start training every day. Pretty soon, you'll start to think, "I can do this." In real estate, you have to go out and put offers on properties. Take calculated risks even if it feels uncomfortable.

At some point, if you take enough action and you follow

your map, you will see results. You can't avoid results. If you have a sound plan and you go out there and do something that has worked before, because duplication is powerful, you're going to get results.

As soon as you start getting results, your belief level skyrockets. It's inevitable. The first property is the hardest, the toughest, and the most anxiety-ridden, but you just keep going, and you do better and better each time.

AS SOON AS YOU START GETTING RESULTS, YOUR BELIEF LEVEL SKYROCKETS.

Soon you'll gain momentum. You'll buy your second property, then your third. Your confidence keeps going up, up, up, and you ride the momentum. You can also kill the momentum if you stop doing what you're doing or if you let other things distract you. Once you have a good momentum pipeline, you just ride it as far as it will go.

Think about what was working against me. I have only a high school education. I'm in a business that most people don't succeed in because of the extreme competition, challenges, and obstacles. I had powerful elements stacked against me. I had an egomaniac who was determined to destroy my company before it started. My capital was tied up. I hadn't done it before. I didn't understand the moving parts. People were naysaying me, telling me not to attempt it because I would fall flat on my face.

I HAD AN EGOMANIAC WHO WAS DETERMINED TO DESTROY MY COMPANY BEFORE IT STARTED.

What helped me achieve success was being able to visualize the company before it even existed, my heartfelt belief that I could build it, dogged perseverance, and just plain old grinding it out. I put one foot in front of the other until I made it happen. That takes fierce mind power.

LIFE IS FULL OF SEVEN-FIGURE DECISIONS

When I was getting threatened, I was told, "You better take your time because you're making a seven-figure decision." That's when a light bulb went on for me. My life had been a series of seven-figure decisions as far back as I can remember. Even when I decided not to pursue college, that was a seven-figure decision, because I knew that wasn't my path to entrepreneurship.

Many people told me that not attending college was the worst decision I'd ever made. A case could be made for that, but I knew college wouldn't get me where I needed to go. I just wasn't wired that way. I was meant to do something else with my life. That was a seven-figure decision because it led me to my business. Otherwise, I still would have been in college at twenty-one years old, pursuing a degree and a job, instead of starting my technology business at a young age, and I would have missed the technology boom. As I said before, life is a game of inches and decisions.

When I got threatened, I had some big decisions to make, and I knew the potentially massive downside. I struggled with the thought, "Is this the right thing to do?" Many people told me, "Are you sure you want to take this on? Are you sure you can handle this? He could put you out of business. What if he gets a judgment against you?" So I had to make that seven-figure decision.

I made it, ultimately, because I convinced myself that I could do it. I forced myself to believe it, despite the challenges in front of me and despite the threats. People told me, "You're putting too much money on the line. You have too many elements against you. You have this guy gunning for you. Just go do properties. You know that business. That's a sure thing for you." Nevertheless, I followed my path and pushed past all the naysayers. I believed with certainty that I was supposed to be in this business, that it was my destiny.

I BELIEVED WITH CERTAINTY THAT I WAS SUPPOSED TO BE IN THIS BUSINESS, THAT IT WAS MY DESTINY.

If I had listened to the naysayers, my whole self-identity today would be different. Instead, I went into absolute crazy beast mode.

BELIEVE YOU CAN DO IT

After I talked to Scott Bell and figured out what I wanted to do, I could never have taken the next steps if I hadn't convinced myself I could do it. Deep down, when someone doesn't believe in something, they don't pursue it. They make excuses for why they shouldn't pursue it. They don't come right out and say, "Hey, you know what? I just don't believe I can do this. I just don't think I have what it takes." People don't admit that. Instead, they rationalize it in their own mind, and they come up with all the excuses for why they shouldn't do it. They think they're making a wise decision, but they're actually making a cowardly one.

THEY THINK THEY'RE MAKING A WISE DECISION, BUT THEY'RE ACTUALLY MAKING A COWARDLY ONE.

As for me, I was forcing myself in my core to believe I could and would do it. I took everything in me that was either negative or derived from fear, and I replaced it with positivity. I replaced it with confidence. Convince yourself that you've already made it and believe it, period.

SELF-DOUBT CAN BE INSIDIOUS

If you're like me and you had no clue what the word *insidious* means when you first heard it or read it, let me help you out.

> ***insidious*** *(adjective) proceeding in a gradual, subtle way, but with harmful effects*

Self-doubt is insidious. In layperson's terms, it means that doubting yourself will slowly sink you and have disastrous effects on your business and your life. Self-doubt is a slow, silent killer.

You have to be aware of self-limiting thoughts sneaking up on you. Some people aren't even aware of them. They just vaguely sort of feel doubt in the back of their mind. That makes them subconsciously shy away from challenges. They won't take a calculated risk, even though they can't put their finger on why. They subconsciously won't face a fear because it just doesn't feel right.

It's like putting your hand close to a light socket; something doesn't feel right, so you pull away from it. However, if you consciously know that you're in the right place and that you're going to be OK, then you can push past it. Pushing past fear will take you to greatness.

Most of the successful people in this world have had to

face difficult challenges, obstacles, people gunning for them, enemies, opposition, roadblocks, and others coveting what they have. That's too much for some people, so they shy away from success. It feels uncomfortable knowing that others are rooting for you to fail, but sometimes you have to accept a little discomfort in order to succeed and win.

When I lost my computer business, I had no idea I was wearing my identity on my sleeve. I didn't know that being a negative and fearful person was blocking my success. I wasn't conscious of these things until my mentor pointed it out to me. Once you're conscious of it, at least you can make informed decisions. You might still choose to do something mediocre, but at least you're making a conscious decision. You're entitled to make your own decisions; just be aware of the subtle forces that are influencing you, especially the insidious ones.

YOU'RE ENTITLED TO MAKE YOUR OWN DECISIONS; JUST BE AWARE OF THE SUBTLE FORCES THAT ARE INFLUENCING YOU, ESPECIALLY THE INSIDIOUS ONES.

CONVINCE YOURSELF

If you're not certain of your own future success, nobody else is going to be, so chances are, it won't happen. You'll stop, or you won't put your full effort in, or you will find excuses to do other things. Your doubts will be accentuated by all the naysayers who don't want you to achieve greatness.

My former partner didn't want me to succeed because it challenged him. He believed that he was the one who owned that training space, who ruled that world. His fatal flaw was that he wanted my failure more than he wanted his own success. He spent more time focused on defeating me than he did running his own business. I was in his head more than his own company was. Instead of focusing on how to turn his business around, he put all of his effort into stopping me. He masked his own greed and responsibility, his fake posturing and ego, but deep down, he must have known that he was failing. He must have known he was losing what he coveted most.

HE SPENT MORE TIME FOCUSED ON DEFEATING ME THAN HE DID RUNNING HIS OWN BUSINESS.

He lost everything that was his identity by trying to make sure that I didn't take a piece of it. Every step of the way, he lost face, whether losing the lawsuit, losing his employees to me, or seeing his reputation getting tarnished. He spent more time threatening his people to keep them from coming to my company than he did trying to keep the people at his company for the right reasons. Everything that he feared happened because he was more focused on the negative, and he lived in constant fear. Every single thing that he wanted to stop by proactively attacking, he created even faster and bigger.

He made a decision to attack me at every level, personally and in business. He made a decision to focus on me. Literally, people in his company would say, "That's all he talked about." I was so in his head. It was unreal.

It didn't have to happen like that, but he made the seven-figure decision to cut ties with me. It was a seven-figure decision based on ego and greed. He made an unethical choice and took something from someone for his own gain. What I want you to see is that focusing on the negative instead of his own success brought his worst fears into reality. Remember that, and don't fall into that trap in your business.

MINDSET IS EVERYTHING

The more successful you are, the more people are gunning for you. You have to be strong mentally. I wasn't in the greatest financial position when I started because my money was tied up. I took a big chance, but that wasn't the real challenge.

My real challenge was the mental game. If I hadn't gotten a hold of my mental game, even if I'd had $10 million to start with, I would never have made this company work. With the mental game in check, I could have done this with fifteen cents. I don't know how, but I would have found a way. That was more important than the financing and all the other components that needed to be put together. Once I had a solid grip on the mental game, I was off and running because I believed it.

WITH THE MENTAL GAME IN CHECK, I COULD HAVE DONE THIS WITH FIFTEEN CENTS.

WORDS HAVE POWER

We speak either blessings or curses on a daily basis to ourselves and to others. Words have power. Maybe you've had people in your life that you looked up to who told you that you can't accomplish big things. They might have said it to you verbally, or they might have communicated it through their actions. It's difficult enough to achieve success, and naysayers make it even harder.

You have to raise the roof of your limitations. Strengthen your mind, plug into networks, and find a mentor who is going in the same direction as you. Don't let the old negative identity reassert itself. Recognize when you're slipping backward or when your environment is having an effect on you, then adjust.

On the first day of my bus tour, Friday, when all of the students first sit in front of me, I spend three hours talking about the mental game. It's all I deal with at first, going over it again and again. I basically tell them, "Listen, for the first few hours, you analytical types are going to be frustrated and wonder why I haven't taught you the real estate system yet. You're going to absorb four days and nights of so much content that you are going to know exactly what to do and how to do it. You're going to have total confidence, but understand something: I could give all of you the same training, but only half of you will do it, and half of you won't.

"Nobody else will tell you that. All the other training companies will try to convince you that you're all going to make millions. They get your emotions inflated, and they set you up for failure. I'm giving you the reality, and the reality is that it's your decision whether or not to succeed at this. The people who make it won't be the smartest or the ones who know all the numbers. I don't know construction as well as the people on my staff who specialize in construction. What put me on this stage, and what got me in front of you, is the stuff I'm talking about right now, fighting through the negative thoughts and fear to where you 100 percent believe you are going to accomplish your vision. Unless you can do that, unless you're aware of it, many of you will go home and fall back into your daily routine. You're going to fall back into the fear, and you're going to make excuses."

I tell them, "Have you ever met somebody who is so book smart that they would be the champ on *Jeopardy*, but they've never turned it into financial success? It's great to have knowledge, but successful people have something that others don't have. That's what we're talking about right now. Unless you learn this, it doesn't matter how good my training is. Many of you won't make it."

SUCCESSFUL PEOPLE HAVE SOMETHING THAT OTHERS DON'T HAVE.

"We're going to talk about this," I say. "We are going to redirect your core, and we're going to do this throughout the weekend. It's not going to be a self-help weekend because self-help without a vehicle is worthless when you are talking about making money. I'm giving you the vehicle, which is the real estate investment strategy. But unless you understand these other principles, you might not be successful. I can tell you why I'm here: it's because I grinded it out and never gave up. I kept pushing. If you can do that, you will be successful. At what level? I don't know. That's up to you. But what we teach you works if you work it."

SKEPTICISM IS NORMAL

When students arrive at one of my bus tours, their knees are knocking. Somehow, they've found the courage to show up. I provide a forty-five-minute audio recording that they listen to before they arrive at my event. Some of them sign up two weeks before; some of them sign up six weeks before. They're excited about the potential. But some of them lose that excitement prior to showing up because they talk to a few people, become nervous, and convince themselves that the decision they made and the journey they are about to go on is a bad idea. Then they want to cancel, or they don't want to come. But the ones who make it arrive with a mixture of excitement and skepticism.

I tell them, "I was in your seat once; I know how you feel. Look, I have eighteen years of law enforcement experience. Everything I did when I was a cop started out as an untruth, and I had to work my way to a truth. You're talking to someone who went through a real estate training system that didn't work. It was broken, and I still made it here. So I understand the skepticism. Some of you have been through other courses, so you're even less likely to believe what I'm saying right now. It's good to trust and verify, but by day four, you're going to see a different class. You're going to see a transformation in this room. I don't care if you believe it or not right now. You're going to see it."

Over the four days, that room goes from a mixture of excitement and skepticism on Friday morning to absolute confidence and excitement on day four. It's not due to pumping music, funky costumes, or dance parties. It's real. By the end, I've given them everything they need: the knowledge, the strategies, a community, a network, systems, and the success principles. As long as they have the mental game right, they're ready.

A STRONG MIND IS A LIFELONG HUSTLE

The process of building a positive mindset is a daily necessity. These principles I'm giving you are something I do daily, especially during the tough times. When you're alone at night, or at three in the morning, and you happen to wake up, that's the witching hour. That's when whatever is good or bad is accentuated in your life. When I was going through my toughest time, that was when the fear and pressures always hit me the hardest. In my mind, I would pray and self-talk, and I would keep envisioning my future success. I would make myself believe it. Obviously, I couldn't speak it out loud at three o'clock in the morning, but I would pattern interrupt it away in my head.

When you pattern interrupt something, it doesn't go away for good. It takes years for all of our baggage to accumulate, so when you try to rid yourself of it, you have a constant battle, even when things are going great. Stuff will resurface, and when it does, you have to hit hard with what you've learned. Every single time I could, I'd either be thinking in my head or saying it out loud, "Bullshit. I am the best in this business. Bullshit. I am the best in this business."

As I said it out loud, it pissed me off because I would start to think about all the stuff that happened to me. Then I would say over and over, "Fuck this. Fuck this. Fuck him. Fuck this. I'm fucking going to build the best training company this industry has ever seen. I am going to win or die trying." That is what it takes when you want something bad enough. That's the mindset you need to take on and then protect.

If somebody was in my way or pointed out some problem, I would literally say, "Bullshit. I'm doing this. You're either part of this, or you're not, and if you're not, shut up and move out of my way, because I'm doing this." I convinced myself, morning, noon, and night, seeing it in my mind and believing it, before I started taking action. Then when I took action, I worked morning, noon, and night like a beast.

THEN WHEN I TOOK ACTION, I WORKED MORNING, NOON, AND NIGHT LIKE A BEAST.

THE VOICES IN YOUR HEAD

Believe me, the fear in my mind reared its head constantly in the early days of my company. Every few minutes, a voice in my head whispered, "You won't make it. You're going to look like an idiot. What if you don't do this? What if you lose the $800,000 you're taking out of your house to fund this? What if they don't release the money they're holding hostage? What if he sues you and he wins?" Anytime that voice whispered, I spoke my belief again. "Bullshit. Other people have overcome more than this. Bullshit. I'm going to become who I'm supposed to be. Bullshit. I'm the best in this business."

When the Devil whispered, "The storm is coming," do you remember what you say back as a warrior? You say, "I am the fucking storm. Now get behind me because I got shit to do."

I am pretty pumped up writing this right now. Just don't forget to fight for what is in your head. You own that space, and you decide what it holds. Trust me, if it's filled with fear and negativity, you own that, nobody else but you. In contrast, if your mind is filled with strong beast-mode thoughts, be proud of that. You earned it.

PARTICIPATION TROPHY, MY ASS

What's the value of telling yourself you're the best at something? It empowers you to become the best. You aren't saying you are the best at everything, and it isn't about being perfect. It's about convincing yourself, in your own head, that there's no second place for you. Why set your limitation to be second best or third best, or to earn a stupid participation ribbon? I want the blue ribbon! So I tell myself I'm going to win the blue ribbon. I'm always shooting for first place.

I'M ALWAYS SHOOTING FOR FIRST PLACE.

Society has made weaklings in my opinion. Not everyone should get a trophy. Trophies need to be earned as a result of performance, not given away for free so someone doesn't feel bad or feel left out. The concept of participation trophies infuriates me because life doesn't work that way. We are sending weak, soft, underperforming kids into a world that doesn't reward participation. The real world will chew you up and spit you out with no apology. As a matter of fact, it will crack you over the head with the first-place trophy on the way out.

My point is that you must earn your success. Be the best or, at least, try to be at all costs. Don't just accept second place; keep looking toward first place. Believe you're the best until you are the best.

BELIEVE YOU'RE THE BEST UNTIL YOU ARE THE BEST.

BE A TWEAKER AND STAY FOCUSED

Keep your eye on the ball and stay focused. If you have something that works, pound it into the ground until it's a carcass. If it stops working, find something else because you always have to evolve. Your cheese is going to be moved. But while it lasts, just go medieval on it.

If you just want to tinker around with real estate as a hobby, that's fine. My goal was different. My goal was to create as much financial security as I could by becoming the best at the cash flow business. I focused on the turnkey, single-family residences because that was the low-hanging fruit in the market. I kept knocking them down, one after the other. That's what you have to do if you want to be the best. Focus on one thing; don't try to be the master of everything.

I tell my students, "When I went into this business, one of the things that resonated with me was the idea of building passive income. I wanted something that would create security, so that was my goal within this vehicle of real estate investing. As I started perfecting my passive income system, gaining momentum, doing forty, fifty, or seventy properties a month within my turnkey system, I avoided making the mistakes that some people make. I didn't lose my focus. I knew what was creating massive revenue and pulling me out of my situation, so I focused on it. I attacked it like a football running back hitting a hole in the defensive line. Like I've said, you see the gap, and you go for it. You hit it hard, and you keep hitting it until it closes up."

Focus and keep perfecting. Even with my cash flow business, it wasn't perfect when I first started. I didn't have the best team, but I kept improving, I kept making the properties better, I kept getting better pricing, I improved my customer service. The same goes for my training company. You wouldn't recognize us from our first event because of all the tweaking and improving we've done since then. Tweak and perfect. Tweak and perfect. Tweak and perfect.

The early training events were good, but I'm always competing with myself. I'm always trying to make things better. It's the right thing to do. You provide customers with a better product.

As I perfected my system, I always leaned on people who knew the business better than I did. I always had mentors. I'm always open to suggestions. I might not agree with the suggestions, but I'm willing to listen. Sometimes the suggestion is right, and I make the adjustment.

I surround myself with people whom I can learn from. Most people who are know-it-alls are insecure. They have to feel like the smartest person in the room, even when they aren't. I don't surround myself with people who are richer or better than I am just because I want to be around successful people. I do it because I want to learn from them and raise my own game.

I want to know how a friend of mine like Kevin Harrington from ABC's *Shark Tank* can be worth $500 million and still have time to create all these new businesses. When I'm with him, I pay attention. I listen because I want to go to his level. I don't want to go to that level because I want to be a hotshot. As I've said before, I want to be financially secure because when you come from a place of abundance, you can help more people.

NEXT STEP: MAP IT

Once you see your vision, once you figure out how to truly believe it, you need a plan—or as I call it, a map. You need a system. You can't go off half-cocked with just a vision and a belief. You're not going to flip a house or start a business if you don't have a set plan, system, or a network in place. Take your vision and belief and put it into a system—ideally, a tried-and-true system that has worked thousands of times before.

One thing that will help you build success faster is great training. You have to surround yourself with people who know how to do it and will show you how to do it. When I started my training company, I had to map it, I had to figure out all the moving parts, and I had to have a system for each of the moving parts.

When you're flipping a property, you have to know the value, you have to know what to offer on a purchase price. You must have it mapped out. You can't haphazardly go after something. You have to have a plan.

CHAPTER TWELVE

—

MAP IT

Take your vision, turn it into a belief, then map out a plan to make that vision a reality. You need a good map to make sure you take calculated risks and understand all the moving parts of your business. It's impossible to know everything, so you will learn some of it along the way. That's fine. But a big-picture, overall game plan is an essential road map to where you want to go.

When I say you need a plan, I mean you have to create an outline and blueprint for exactly what you are going to do. People who come to my training receive all the education they need, but then they have to take that information and create a written blueprint for their own company. That's exactly what I did when I started my training business. I mapped out the steps I needed to take.

You can't just take the training you receive, throw it against a wall, and see what sticks. This is your financial life after all. Many people and partners are depending on you, so you have to know what comes next. You need to know each step.

For example, in a property deal, you have to know what to offer on a purchase price, and you have to know the value of the property after it's rehabbed. If you go in blindly without a plan, your offers won't be accepted. You have to know how to find a property and how to sell it, so you need to map out every step. I'm a big proponent of using a proven system.

Mapping your plan ensures you know what to do and in what order. You can take your vision and believe in it all you want, but if you don't know what steps to take, everything is just one big risk. You don't need an exact plan, because much will change as you proceed, but without clarifying the steps, your actions will be reckless.

COME UP WITH A REAL PLAN

To create the framework for my company, I consulted with Scott Bell. He gave me a basic outline of the steps to take. However, the core of my business was based off my own experience, particularly the negative experiences I had as a student in 2004. I learned what not to do as a result of the costly mistakes I made then. And of course, watching Montenegro run his training company into the ground was a good map of what not to do. In one of my depositions, they asked me if I copied his business model. My answer was, "No. I did exactly the opposite so my company would succeed and last."

I knew the hustle. I knew how the industry operated. And I vowed to do things differently for my students and to establish a better reputation. That required mapping out the training and making sure that students would go home and know how to take their first step and make their first move.

I wanted my training to be up to date, to be packed with useful tips, to have no fluff, and to give specific information so students would know how to act and what to do. My company was never going to take advantage of them by sending them away without being the best in the business and having a specific plan to execute.

YOUR NETWORK IS YOUR NET WORTH

Part of my training business map, and one of the missing pieces that I didn't get from the training I took, was a real network and community. I believe in the saying "Your network is your net worth," so I created a network for my highest-level students on Facebook. It now has thousands of members. It's growing fast, and every member of the group is trained at the same high level. They all know how to make a plan, execute it, and put together good deals.

Some of those students don't have a lot of money yet, but they offer their time and knowledge. Others don't have much time, but they have financial resources. It's a network where people can partner and invest in safety, offering deals only within the community. I teach them to go slow, flipping one or two houses at first, and they're getting strong deals accepted. I knew this was a missing piece, and I mapped out how this would work for my students.

I teach them not to pass up good deals but to wholesale them within the network for a fee. It's a win for everyone. Somebody makes a few bucks by finding a great property and putting together all the information, then somebody else pays a small fee and makes a nice profit by flipping it.

Within the network, students are wholesaling to one another, funding each other's deals, partnering, problem solving, and encouraging one another. They were all taught the same system, so they know how it works, and they're operating out of the same playbook. Most of my instructors and mentors are on there to answer basic questions as well, although I have hotlines for the complicated questions. For light questions and answers and support, I personally engage with the group every single day. For our advanced graduates who complete the higher levels of training, we also assign each student a phone coach and personal mentor, but the Facebook group keeps them plugged into the community.

If students paid their tuition just to be in that group, it would be worth every penny because they're doing millions of dollars' worth of real estate deals together. They all have the same mission. I can't micromanage it, of course, but I teach my students from the stage that they must do business ethically. Mistakes will be made, some deals will be challenging, but students must communicate and treat one another with respect.

For most real estate training companies, once a student has paid and finished the course, the company is done with them and on to the next batch of students. We don't operate like that. I tell my students, "We are going to know each other for a long time. You're going to be part of this network for years to come." If any changes or redirection happen in the market, they'll be part of it.

If my students become successful, it reflects better on me. The reputation of my company is everything, so when students are successful, I'm successful. I don't have any negative pushback or bad press because we do what we say, and I'm real with people.

I built the network map with a set of very detailed guidelines and implemented it with precision.

DAILY RITUALS

Part of creating a plan involves mapping out the specific daily rituals and actions. This is the key to success because success is rooted in the small stuff that happens every day. When I first started, I had a plan, and I stuck to it. Even now, I stay disciplined and follow my map every day.

In my life, I don't let minutiae slow me down or stand in my way. If you have to make twenty offers a day because that's what it's going to take for you to be successful, then sit down and make the offers. If you have to call a certain number of contractors a day, sit down and call them. It doesn't matter what else you have going on, unless it's an emergency. Students are so excited about their business, but then they waste two weeks trying to figure out how to design the best business card.

I know it's exciting to come up with a logo. It needs to be done, and you can be proud of it. But honestly, forget about your business card and focus on the things that will bring about results. Do the things that you're supposed to do to create revenue, because when you create revenue, everything works better. When you have money coming in, you can pay someone else to do the minutiae for you.

If someone asks you to help them move because you're a friend and you own a truck, give them $200 to hire a mover so you can keep working and making your offers. Don't get drawn into meaningless time wasters. In my business, I have people doing things in different departments, and I don't micromanage them. Now, when something breaks, I go back and focus on it. I figure out why it's broken and spend time fixing it. But as soon as it's fixed, I go back to focusing on the things that create revenue.

I don't focus on our computer system or the call center we have or decorating my office. I focus on the things that will generate momentum for the company. That includes creating new brands, working on marketing, or, when I'm in the real estate business, making offers.

If you need to fix your CRM software or fancy up your website, have someone else do that for you. If you can't find someone else to do it, then go ahead and tackle it yourself, but hurry and move on. You have more important things to work on. Take steps every day to create revenue for yourself.

GOOD VERSUS BAD HABITS

Following a set map will help you develop better habits. People have certain daily rituals, both good habits and bad. Examine yourself and see what your daily rituals are. Ask yourself, "Are my habits consistent with my map for my business? Have my habits put me in my current situation?" If you're in a great position, keep doing more of that. If you're in a bad position, then it's time to stop the patterns that contribute to it. Change your habits so that you're moving in the right direction every day. You have to be honest with yourself about this.

Do more of the daily rituals and actions that are going to create momentum for you, move you forward in your plan, and generate results. Any habit that doesn't do that needs to be shelved, at least until you achieve certain milestones. If it's a leisure activity, you can shelve it for now, then find time for it later on when you've achieved success.

I believe that if you took all the money away from successful people, after a certain time, those same people would acquire wealth all over again. That's because they make plans, and they have a set of principles and actions they take every day that moves them in the right direction. They have a good plan, confidence, the right mindset, and the right focus.

When it comes to unsuccessful people, they tend to do the same things over and over, thinking that one of these days, they'll see different results. Some say that's the definition of insanity; I say it's the definition of stupidity. If your actions aren't producing the results you want, you have to change. If certain actions keep creating failure, figure out what those actions are and change them. Replicate only what works.

If something works for someone else, take those actions and incorporate them into your daily routine. Duplication is powerful. There's power in doing the daily things that make you successful versus the things that don't. Over time, those daily actions add up to big success.

I've had to do things that took tremendous discipline and willpower. I've had to take actions that were painful, either because of the fear involved or because of the difficulty and time commitment. But I can tell you for certain what feels far worse is regret over the actions I never took. When you fail to take action out of fear, the regret stays with you forever. The pain of all the carnage I went through at my lowest point hardly matters because it led me to success. Temporary pain builds long-term gain that leads to success.

The stuff I failed to do in my life because of fear, that's the source of real pain. That regret is hard to shake off. The pain of discipline is ounces; the pain of regret is tons.

THE PAIN OF DISCIPLINE IS OUNCES; THE PAIN OF REGRET IS TONS.

THE BIGGEST CHALLENGE LIES AHEAD: EXECUTING

I never planned to start my own training company. I had every intention of staying in my lane and expanding my cash flow business. Only when I was forcibly removed from that position did I consider a different lane. This unfortunate situation helped me to see what I was supposed to be doing, but it only happened because I was forced out. Once I had a new vision, however, I put together my plan with help from Scott, and then it was time to take action.

Once you have a plan, once you've mapped out the steps, it's time to execute it. That's the hardest challenge. To do that, I had to face financial challenges and overcome legal and emotional obstacles that were gut-wrenching. But I did it because I knew that without proper execution, my vision, belief, and plan are worthless.

—

CHAPTER THIRTEEN

EXECUTE IT

Now that you have a plan, you have to start doing something. Many people stall out at this stage of the game, where the rubber hits the road. They reach a point where they experience a complete stutter. For me, it happened when I had to fund my new business. I had to take out more debt and put leveraged money on the line.

EXECUTING IS YOUR "OH SHIT" MOMENT

Executing your plan and actually following the map you created is the scariest part of starting a business, but you mustn't hesitate. Opportunity comes and goes, so you have to take calculated risks while you can. As long as you have all of the pieces in place, take action. If you struggle to make an offer or start that business, if you're overthinking it or wasting time, the opportunity will disappear.

True leaders, true entrepreneurs, and successful people are able to move past this stage. They execute their plan, and that's why they achieve success. I worked morning, noon, and night to map out my strategy, and finally game time arrived. That's when you find out what you're made of. Taking that first step forward is the toughest.

I know too many people who make great plans but spend years waiting to take the first step in execution. They're always cooking up the next great idea, but they never achieve anything because they don't take action. They never have more than a good idea, a nice thought, an interesting dream.

OPPORTUNITY DOESN'T WAIT FOR YOU

If you have a bunch of deals and you know the numbers work but you can't make yourself pull the trigger, you're going to miss out. While you keep thinking about it, someone else is going to make an offer or start that business. This kind of missed opportunity is prevalent in real estate.

Often, the window of opportunity is limited. When I started my training company, I needed to launch by January 2014, which meant I had to pull my program together quickly. If I'd kept thinking, analyzing, and messing around with logos, I would have rolled into summer, which is the slowest time of the year for real estate training. That would have harmed the launch of my company.

As long as you have the right plan, go out there and take action. Make offers. On the microlevel, you can miss an individual deal if you don't act. On the macrolevel, you can miss a shift in the entire market. Hindsight is always twenty-twenty. I hear people say, "The best time to invest in real estate was back in 2009, so maybe I shouldn't do it now." Well, ten years from now, you'll wish you'd started investing in 2018. You can't take action without making a decision, and making no decision is itself a decision, and it's the worst decision you can make.

In the last four years, I've made many bad decisions regarding my company. When I take a step back and take a look at it, I acknowledge I've missed the mark here and there. It happens, but it's not the end of the world. At least you are taking action. When I make a bad decision, I just make another decision to fix it. You won't always make the right decision, but it's better to make some wrong decisions and correct them than to make no decision at all. Not making a decision gets you nowhere.

MAKING NO DECISION IS ITSELF A DECISION, AND IT'S THE WORST DECISION YOU CAN MAKE.

PUSH THROUGH ADVERSITY OR BE AVERAGE

I had every single thing stacked against me. My money was being held hostage by my former partner so he could force me to sign an agreement to indemnify him of everything. I had to leverage my house for $800,000 to launch the business. I had to do all of the marketing myself, and I knew nothing about the business. I had people telling me, "You're insane. Who's going to show up to your events? It makes no sense. You're doing this for all the wrong reasons."

I knew I wasn't doing it for the wrong reasons. I was doing it because I knew it was my destiny. Teaching people is what I'm supposed to be doing. My nemesis had already threatened me in 2013, telling me to crawl back under the rock where he found me. He said he would dismantle me financially and personally if I didn't go away. On top of that, I didn't know if my business was going to be profitable out of the gate.

I could write fifty pages about the uphill battle I had in front of me, but the bottom line is, this became a defining moment for me. I decided I didn't want to look at myself in the mirror someday and feel ashamed that I'd run the other way out of fear. I wanted to look in the mirror and see a beast, not a coward. I decided I was going to take hold of my destiny.

The more I was attacked, the more he breached my events to have me served, and the more employees he threatened with lawsuits, the more I had to spend to defend and protect my business. Did I have moments of doubt? Sure. I had moments when I considered signing that agreement. But I knew deep down that I wouldn't be as great if I didn't stand up to the challenge and take a stand. Did I want to be average, or did I want to be the best and win? That was the big seven-figure decision I had to make. I decided to take action and win.

I DECIDED TO TAKE ACTION AND WIN.

BE A LION OR A LAMB—YOU DECIDE

Sometimes you can't stand on principle. Sometimes you have to do what's best for your business, and you need to make pragmatic decisions. You can't let pride stop you. I've made a million of those kinds of good business decisions, but this situation I went through was different. It was personal, and my identity was on the line. The more I was attacked, the more resilience it built in me. I refused to fail, and I refused to break. It burned a massive fire inside of me.

Once I made my decision to fight, I stood by it, and I knew it was right. I believe my company today is as strong as it is because it was born out of adversity. It made me a beast, literally a beast. I fought and worked hard every single day. That's something I still do to this day. Would I want to go through it again? No, but I wouldn't change it for anything. Without that adversity, I wouldn't know what I'm capable of.

I want you to understand that when I tell you to take action, I'm not just saying it. I have chosen to take action in the face of every kind of threat and discouragement. I know what it feels like to stare up at a mountain in your way that has to be climbed. I've lived it, so I'm not asking you to do anything I haven't done myself. If I could take action during that time, in light of what I was up against, I don't see any reason for other people to make excuses.

THERE'S JUST NO WAY AROUND HARD WORK

I attribute all of this success to execution, which is another word for hard work. I worked harder in the months leading up to our launch than I'd ever worked before. I went against the grain and followed my gut, just like I did when I appeared on those radio shows. I became the number one real estate show in Los Angeles because I followed my instincts.

When I designed my company, my teams were trained properly, and the messaging was spot-on and congruent throughout my whole company. I tossed out all the industry nonsense and worthless fluff, and my students appreciate it. Many of them tell me, "There's something different about this program. From the infomercial, all the way through to the first event, second event, and the bus tours, there's something sincere and legit about this. It's what we hoped it would be."

It won't be easy. It's not like the movie *Rocky*, where the music plays and suddenly everything happens. Building a successful business takes weeks, months, and years of scrapping, grinding, and dealing with one challenge after the other.

"PRAY AS IF IT'S UP TO GOD. WORK AS IF IT'S UP TO YOU."

—SAINT AUGUSTINE

If you happen to get lucky and you score big on your first real estate deal, that's great, but life generally doesn't work that way. Success comes with a lot of effort and some pain. I had to eat a lot of dirt to make it to where I am. I didn't always have a clear path, but I persevered, and you will too.

I've seen many students show up with all kinds of baggage and heartache. You might be going through a divorce, you might have bad credit, or you might have someone trying to make you fail. So what? It doesn't matter. All that matters is what you're going to do next. If you map out your plan and work hard to execute it, you will succeed.

When I was starting this business, I worked morning, noon, and night. Just like Michael Jordan practiced harder than anyone, I worked this business harder than anyone. I continue to do so. That's why I'm still the best and why my company's reputation is impeccable. Success begins and ends with hard work.

What you do, what you say, and what you think will be your tomorrow. That you can count on.

WHAT YOU DO, WHAT YOU SAY, AND WHAT YOU THINK WILL BE YOUR TOMORROW. THAT YOU CAN COUNT ON.

FOCUS ON WHAT MAKES YOU MONEY

I am going to be a bit redundant here because I need the readers to really hear this. Another big part of my success is that I knew what to focus on. I don't worry about minutiae. I'm a decision maker, but I delegate. I put capable people in charge of specific areas of my business, people who I know can handle it. Once I do that, I don't micromanage them. I don't have to pound every nail or sign every document.

In the beginning of your business, you might not be able to delegate because you don't have the resources or enough people around you. However, at some point, it's worth it to pay people to do the small stuff so you can focus on creating revenue. Go make offers, and pay someone else to design your business card.

If you don't make any offers, no offers will be accepted. If you don't have any offers accepted, you don't rehab anything. If you don't rehab anything, you don't put anything on the market to sell. If you don't sell, you can't make a profit. It's as simple as that. Focus on creating revenue, and let other people take care of the rest. Don't be sidetracked by chores.

If you want to be successful, there's a price to pay. You might have to say no to playing on the softball team or taking that vacation, especially in the early days of your business. Don't neglect your family, of course, but understand that some sacrifices have to be made while you're focused on launching your business.

Set the right priorities. Why is this business important to you? If you say, "I do it for my kids," then ask yourself, are you kids important enough for you to give up your softball league? Get your act together and focus. Do you really need to sit on the couch every night, drinking a six pack, and watching *Game of Thrones*?

Don't get me wrong, everyone needs time for relaxation and rest. We weren't put on this earth just to work, work,

work. I enjoy my downtime. I look forward to smoking a cigar or a juicy high-stakes poker game. But I find that downtime is most enjoyable after I've earned it by working like a beast. You have to earn it first.

I FIND THAT DOWNTIME IS MOST ENJOYABLE AFTER I'VE EARNED IT BY WORKING LIKE A BEAST. YOU HAVE TO EARN IT FIRST.

Many of the people who fail at this do so because they don't focus on the things that make money. Even if you have to hump a job for forty hours a week at first so you can pay the bills, do it. During your off time, spend time with your loved ones, of course, but also carve out time to make offers. Make offers at night after your kids go to bed. Make them early in the morning before the family wakes up. If you want to succeed, do whatever you have to do. You'll reach a point where you can live the life of your dreams, but you'll never get there if you don't take action and execute your plan.

I don't have a business card. I don't need one. They're just really not that important. These days, we do everything online. I focus on the things that are important and can move the needle. I refuse to engage in insignificant busy-work that might take up a lot of my time. Some people are obsessive-compulsive, and they need to take care of every small task before they can focus on the big stuff. If that's you, you have to find a way around it. I have that kind of personality too, but I force myself to keep my eye on the ball.

DELEGATE AND FOCUS ON REVENUE

More redundancy—sorry, you need to get this. Don't ask me to do yard work on the weekend; I'm not going to do it. It's a running joke in my family. It's not that I'm too good for yard work; it's because I can pay someone else to do it. I could pay someone $40 a week to run all of my errands. There are people who will gladly do it. When you flip a bunch of houses or create revenue from that other business you started, you'll be able to hire people to do your busy work too.

Some people make the mistake of thinking, "I'll do my own yard work and wash my own car because it will save me $100." But it will also take up six hours of your time, which would be better spent focusing on your business. You could make forty-five offers in the time it takes to mow the yard and wash the car. If one of those offers is accepted and you flip that house, you might make $40,000. The math is pretty easy here. Apply this to any business, not just real estate investing.

Of course, in the beginning, when you don't have a lot of money, you might have to do many small tasks yourself, but be careful. Make sure your priorities are not out of whack. People spend more time planning vacations than they do their financial futures. Most people don't focus on creating a business that could change their entire lives, but they will spend weeks trying to save $300 on a vacation. That doesn't make any sense to me. Don't spend your time on three-figure decisions; spend it on seven-figure decisions.

DON'T SPEND YOUR TIME ON THREE-FIGURE DECISIONS; SPEND IT ON SEVEN-FIGURE DECISIONS.

Once you're in a better financial position, you'll be able to take all kinds of vacations. In fact, you'll be able to take the vacations you really want to take, rather than the budget vacations that you can barely afford now. Once you have enough passive income, you can drive the car that you want to drive and not one that you have to drive. You can go take a nap in the middle of the day if that's what you want to do (one of my personal favorites).

Because I focused on building my business, I was one of the only dads who was always at the field day for my girls. I went on their field trips and spent time with them because I'd put myself in a financial position to do that. They are my priority, so I've made time for them. I couldn't have done that if I had to work eight to five every day.

Again, there's nothing wrong with working eight to five if you have to do that. But as I said before, I'll work eighty hours a week to not work forty. Often, I wind up working harder than most people anyway, but it's by choice. I feel good about it; it's not work to me.

FOLLOW THROUGH AND KNOW YOUR BUSINESS AND YOUR MARKET

When it comes to executing, many people don't finish what they start. They begin a lot of things, but they give up long before completion. For example, they might start rehabbing a property, but then they start ten more rehabs and take their eye off the first one. Or they become distracted and lose interest.

Surround yourself with people who are conscientious and follow through. Make sure they have the same goals as you. That way, you will encourage one another to focus on revenue and finish the task at hand.

In real estate, strategies have to change. Markets go up and down, so staying informed is important. I tell people, "You can make money in a down market, you can make money in an up market, and you can make money in a flat market. You just have to be willing to change your strategy to meet the changing market."

Some industries dry up, and when that happens, you must

change and bail out. What if your business was selling fax machines? What if you insisted on continuing to sell fax machines? That would have been a recipe for failure. The people who built businesses selling fax machines had to change at some point. Industries change, markets change, and you have to stay on the cutting edge.

APPRECIATE AND PROTECT WHAT YOU HAVE WHEN YOU HAVE IT

When I started my technology business, I didn't have a real passion or love for technology. I failed to appreciate what I had because I didn't know it could all go away at any time. When it did, I learned a big lesson about how things can change really fast.

Then I had my cash flow business, and that was taken away from me. Success is fleeting. Today, for the first time in my life, when I stand on stage in front of hundreds of cheering students, I fully appreciate what I have. I marvel that I got here at all, and I know it won't last forever. But as long as it lasts, I'm going to enjoy the ride because I love what I do. I love running this business and watching students succeed.

I'M GOING TO ENJOY THE RIDE BECAUSE I LOVE WHAT I DO. I LOVE RUNNING THIS BUSINESS AND WATCHING STUDENTS SUCCEED.

I have enjoyed so much success financially that I don't think I could make enough mistakes at this point to put myself in a bad position. But you never want to get cocky; always appreciate what you have. Success is sweeter now because of what I went through. I protect it more than I ever did before, and I take nothing for granted.

I took my computer business for granted, and I took my cash flow business for granted. But I don't take my new company for granted. On the contrary, I pay attention to it on a minute-by-minute basis. I put everything I have into it, emotionally and physically, and I enjoy every second of it.

PRACTICE WHAT YOU PREACH

Everything I've written about in this book I've personally experienced. Everything I tell students to do, every piece of advice I give, comes from something I've experienced and learned along the way. I don't ask students to do something I didn't do myself, and I don't ever talk about any of the points in this book purely out of theory. Everything in these pages comes from my personal experience.

Prior to taking the stage, I command my mind. Before I teach students on a bus tour, I hunker down for a good week and a half, and I marinate. I go over each section that I know like the back of my hand so I can make sure I don't forget the message. I don't allow myself to become complacent or give the students only 85 percent. They deserve 100 percent, and I give it to them. It's important to me.

Peak states don't just happen; you have to create them and then keep them going. They don't come from luck. They come from constantly working, both behind the scenes and in front of the students. In the end, I'm not competing with another person; I'm competing with my own capabilities. I always try to outdo myself and raise my limitations. I strive to go places I never thought I could go.

PEAK STATES DON'T JUST HAPPEN; YOU HAVE TO CREATE THEM.

If something challenges me, I want to do it. If something intimidates me but I know it's a good decision, I go for it. I refuse to rest on my laurels. People ask me when I plan to retire. I'm fifty-two now, and I don't ever want to retire. Why would I? So I can go sit on a boat and wait for a fish to bite a hook? I love my family, and I will love my grandchildren, but do I want to just sit on the porch and watch them run around? Hell no. I want to keep working, achieving, and doing things. I love the feeling of winning. I want to always feel alive.

I want to continue doing what I love until I can't do it anymore. I have enough money to walk away right now and do whatever the hell I want, but honestly, I don't have the desire to. I don't do this for the money.

What's important to me is to be alive, to feel what I'm feeling, and to continue giving back to the students. I want to create something better than anything that's ever been created in this industry. Ten years from now, maybe my business won't be this training company anymore. Maybe I'll be doing something else, but I definitely won't be sitting on a boat. I'm just not wired like that.

I go on vacations because I love my family, and we enjoy our time together. For myself, I don't enjoy vacations. I need to be stimulated mentally and be hustling. I take a lot of heat for this, but I have to be who I am, or I am nothing.

I don't think I'm a different person at this level of success, because I've had many levels of success in my life. When I had a technology company with one hundred employees and $40 million in revenue, I could have deemed myself successful. I could have declared myself successful when I had my cash flow business in 2013. I was making millions of dollars and doing hundreds of properties.

The difference between then and now is that I love what I'm doing now more than ever. I appreciate it more because of how hard it was to get here. Do I have a nice car? Yes. If you come to my house, you'd probably figure out that I'm doing well financially. However, on a daily basis, I wear a pair of jeans, generally with holes in them, a black T-shirt, and Converse Chuck Taylor sneakers. If you ever see me in a nice suit, it's because I've been indicted. I don't need expensive things to prove my success, and I'm not driven by the money. I enjoy having enough money to experience freedom. I enjoy being able to help other people with my abundance.

Most of all, I appreciate what I have now and what it took to get it. I recognize the blessing this time. Men in suits look really successful until you find out they work for the man in the T-shirt and jeans.

MEN IN SUITS LOOK REALLY SUCCESSFUL UNTIL YOU FIND OUT THEY WORK FOR THE MAN IN THE T-SHIRT AND JEANS.

CONCLUSION

HAVE THE BALLS TO WIN—
IT'S WORTH IT

I have a high school, K–12 education. I didn't go to college. I struggled with academics. Maybe I just didn't fit in the box, or maybe school just wasn't my thing. I didn't come from money; in fact, I didn't come from anything whatsoever. I've never been the smartest guy in the room, but I do have one big advantage over most people: I know how to play to my strengths. My biggest strength is my will to win by pure grit.

Grit.

The reason I am successful is because I don't give up. I'm willing to eat dirt and then bounce back. Even though it doesn't taste good, failure motivates me to do better.

Nobody likes to go through trials and tribulations, but along the way, that perseverance is the difference between those who succeed and those who don't.

Yes, some people catch lucky breaks. Yes, sometimes things fall into place perfectly. But most successful people have failed and failed and failed along the way to success. Most of them have overcome numerous obstacles because they had the courage to keep pushing. That is the definition of grit.

Sometimes when I'm standing in front of four hundred or five hundred students at one of my main events, everything I've gone through to get there runs through my mind like a movie. It's so surreal that I shake my head in amazement. The journey to get here was brutal and gut-wrenching, but I know up on that stage is the place I was meant to be. I am now financially free and doing what I love to do. How I got here is what I'm most proud of.

I have this moment all to myself as I share my story with the students. After four days together, most of the students understand, but nobody fully comprehends what the journey was like. Even after reading this detailed account, you won't really know what I had to do and what I felt during my journey. You can do your best to explain your journey to people, but only you truly know what it felt like to live through it. Looking back, I know it was all worth it. Every single punch I took was worth it to arrive where I am today.

I am so incredibly glad I didn't give up and walk away.

I will leave you with this. No matter what, I hope this book has encouraged and helped you to have the balls to succeed and win in business and in life.

NICK VERTUCCI

NV

ABOUT THE AUTHOR

NICK VERTUCCI went from rags to riches, back to rags, and to riches once more. When his original tech business went under, he made a 180-degree turn to real estate investing, and later began training others to get rich by buying real estate. Currently one of the most in-demand speakers and educators in the real estate investment business, he has built a multimillion-dollar empire that has enabled thousands of students to create enormous wealth.

Made in the USA
San Bernardino, CA
05 August 2018